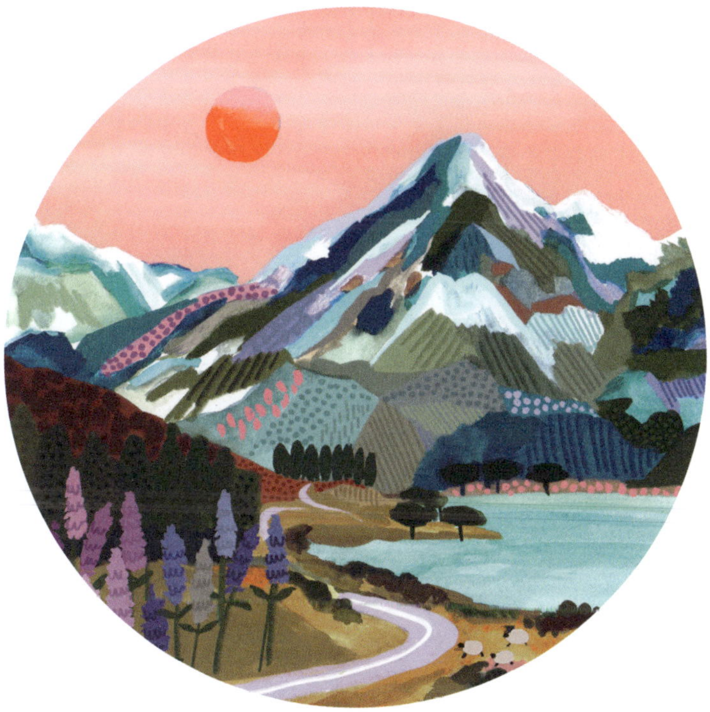

PAINT BY NUMBERS

Art Escapes

Creative landscapes to color in

RHI JAMES OF HEBE STUDIO

Quadrille

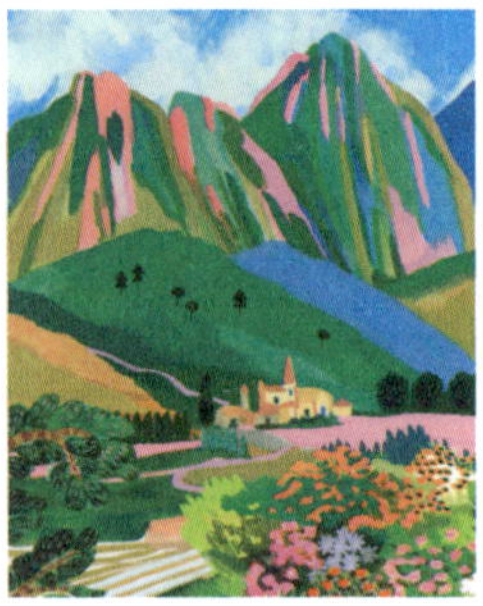

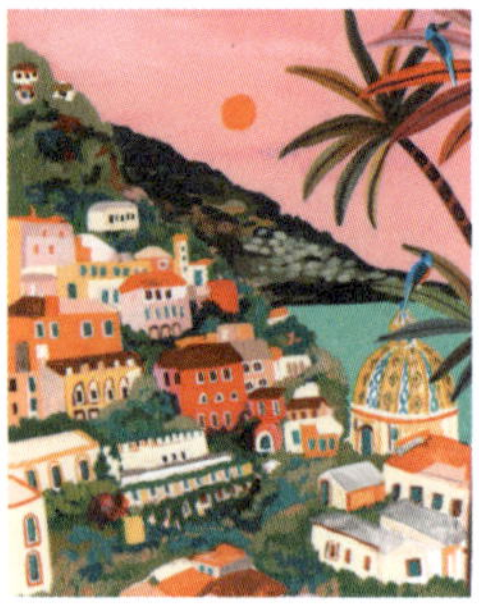

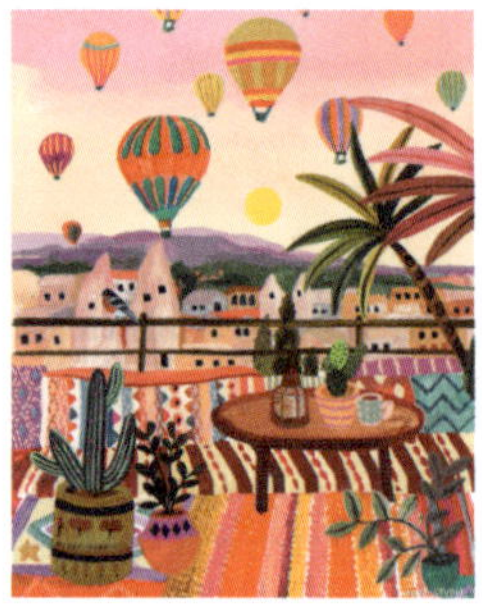

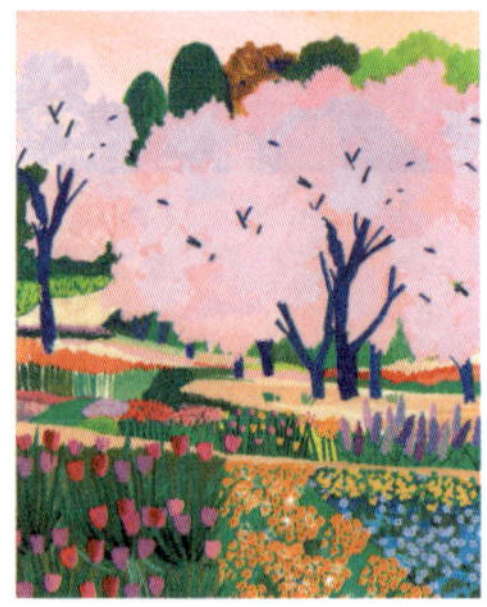

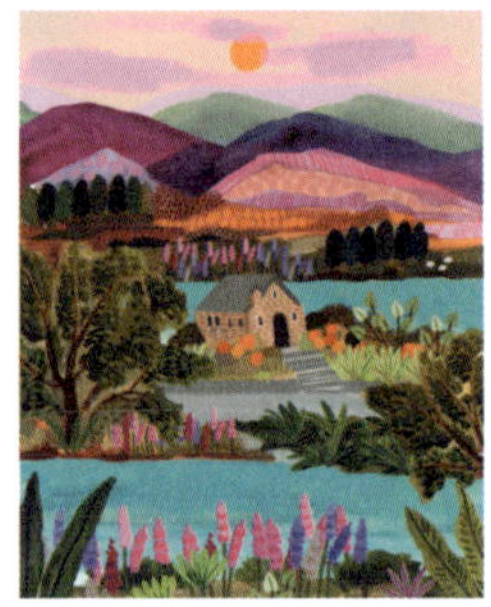

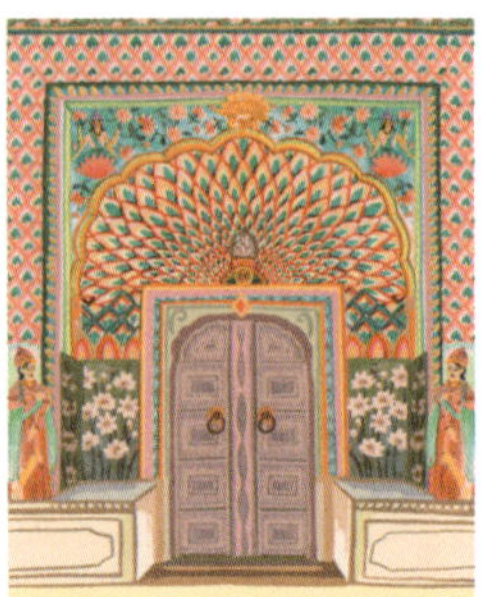

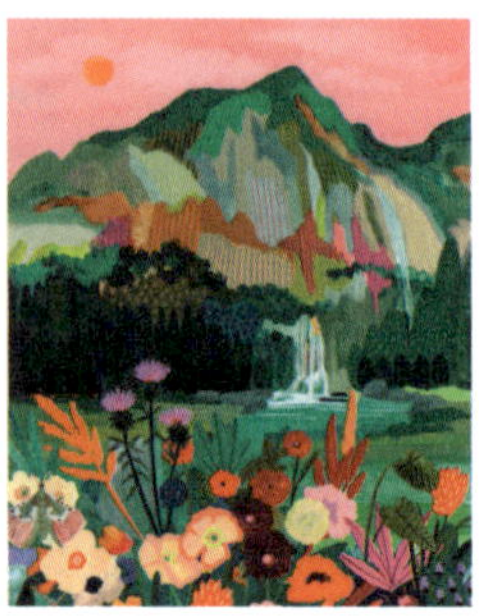

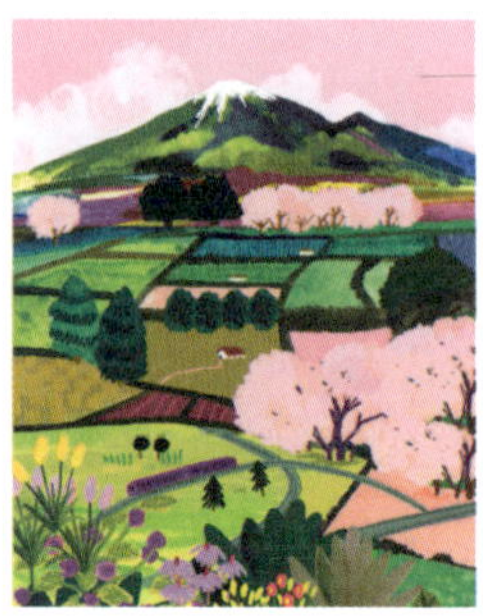

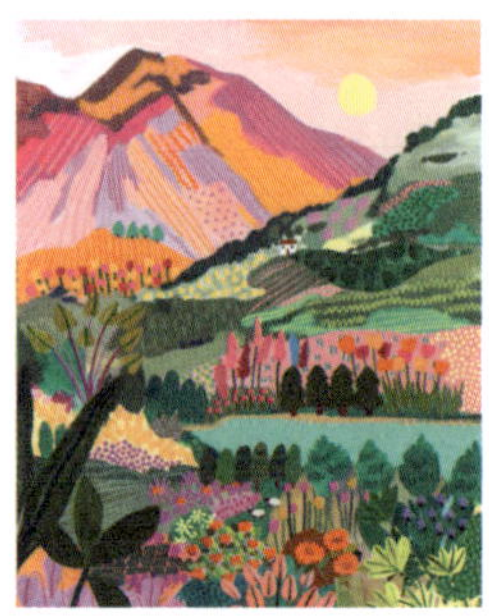

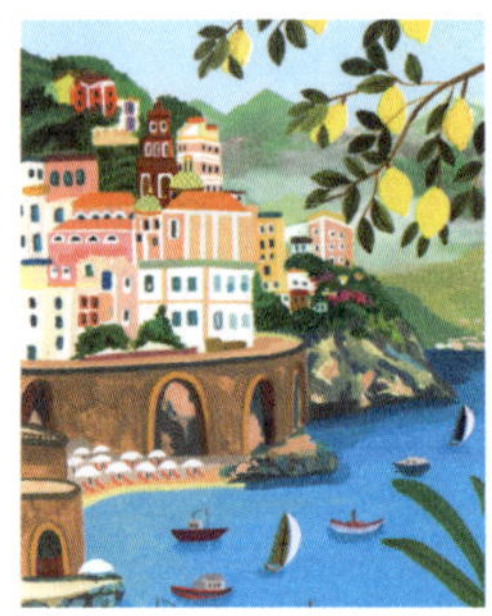

Introduction

Hi, I'm Rhi and I'm an artist and designer. I also love to travel. The book you're now holding in your hands is my way of sharing that passion for art and travel with you.

We all know how magical it is to go on vacation and immerse ourselves in new landscapes, look out onto a stunning view from a balcony, stroll along the beach, walk down a cobbled street lined with the prettiest flowers... We always want to record those precious memories so that we can revisit them on dull days back home, weeks later.

Art Escapes is a sourcebook, a collection of the most beautiful vistas that have inspired me over years of travel. You may have experienced these escapes yourself; you may come across an unknown one that captures your imagination and immediately goes on your bucket list. No matter what your motivation is in pausing at a particular picture in these pages, there's something very special waiting for you: the opportunity to put your phone away, get some paints out, make yourself comfortable and create a lovely piece of art of your own, with my gentle guidance.

Because this is painting by numbers, the complexities of color composition have been taken care of for you, and you just need to consult the swatches, follow the steps and numbered sections on the template, and relax into it.

There are 20 pictures for you to paint, ranging from an iconic view of the Eiffel Tower on a golden evening in Paris; a train ride through the vibrant patchwork landscape of rural Japan, dominated by the majestic Mount Fuji; all the way to Lake Tekapo in New Zealand where the water is a heavenly turquoise and the little building in the middle is possibly the most stunningly located church in the world. There's so much to discover.

I use Winsor & Newton watercolors and gouache paints but you can use whatever medium you prefer for your own artwork – paint, markers, pencils or a combination of all three. Vibrant tones work best, as you'll see from the color swatches I include with each picture. This will also help each section of the picture to stand out and for the overall effect to have that impact we're after. But remember, art is personal and everyone's style is different. You can use the templates in this book and reproduce my paintings very accurately, even if you're a complete beginner at painting. I've made it as easy as possible for you to get great results. However, if you vary the tones, or the paint medium, or experiment with the details of a scene, that's OK too. It's your art, and your escape – make it your own!

I like to think that the process of creating art is as mindful and rewarding as going away on holiday. It's an uplifting activity for quiet afternoons, a way of focussing on something beyond the responsibilities of everyday life. I hope you enjoy the process as much as I do, and if you want to show me your pictures on social media or you have any questions, I always love to hear from you! @hebe.studio

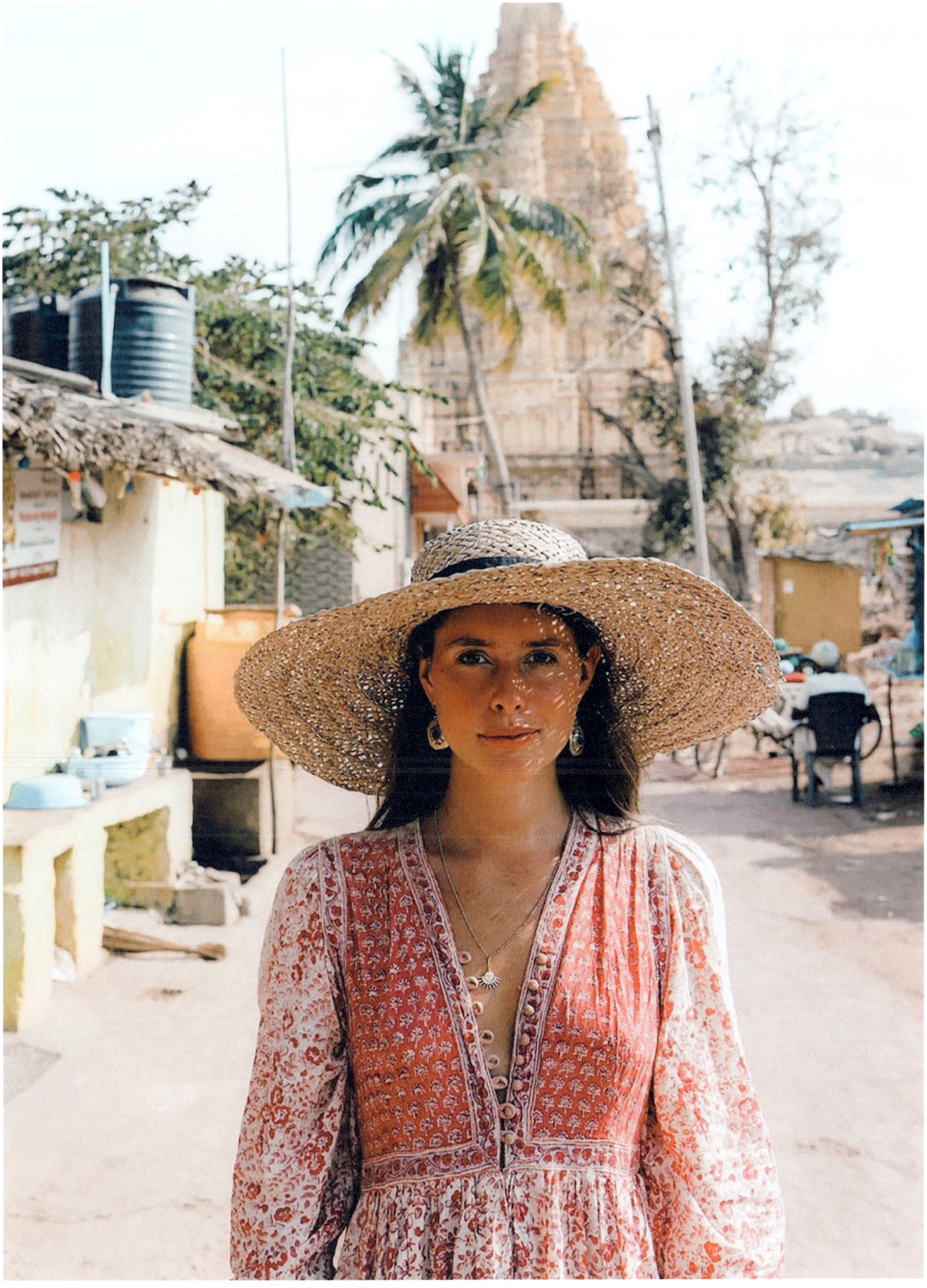

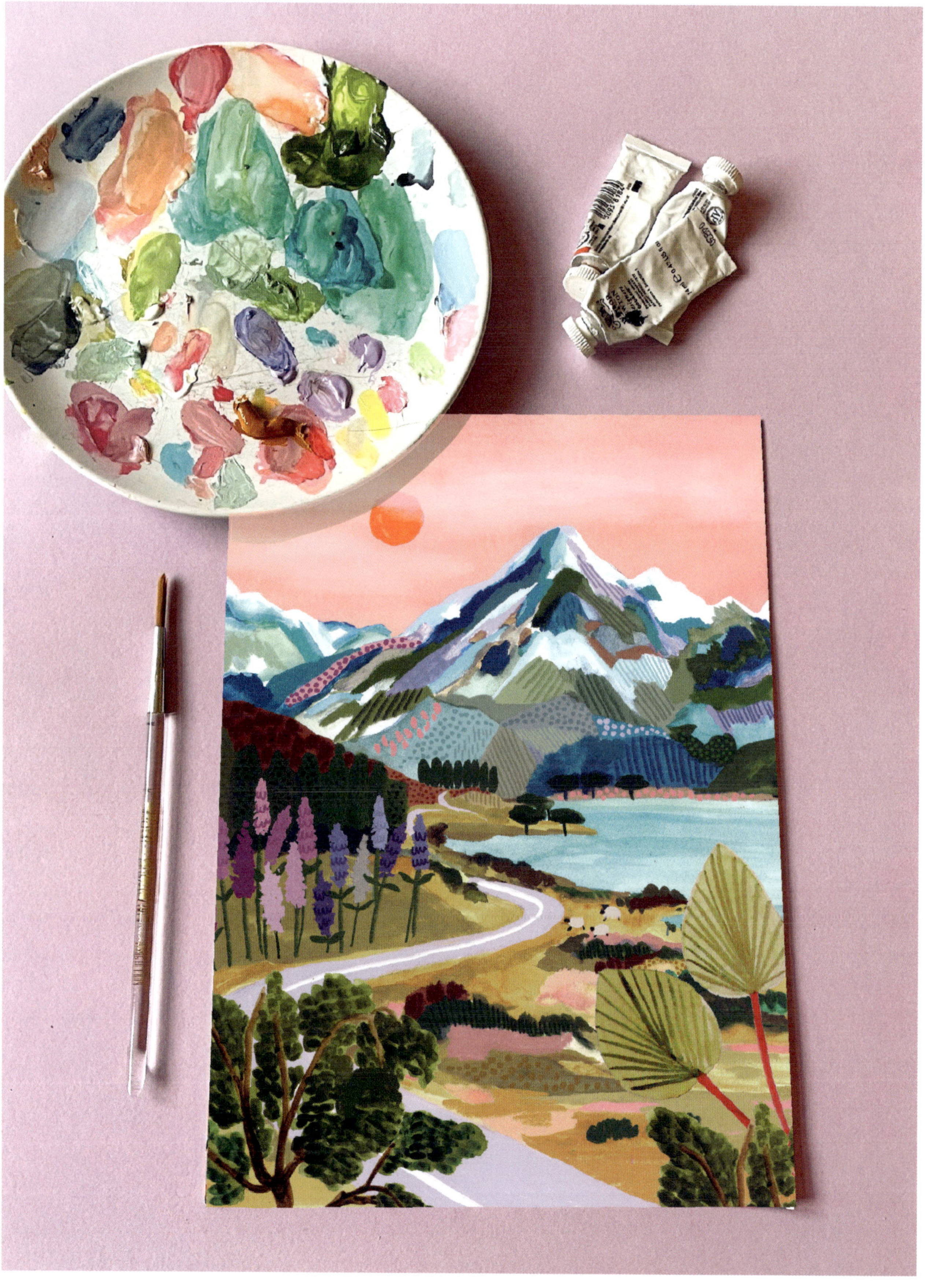

How to use this book

This book is designed to transport you to sunny, faraway places – an invitation to escape as you bring each page to life with color.

The next few pages will walk you through tools and techniques, as well as how to care for your brushes and find inspiration when painting. I want this book to be an invitation to explore the world through color and capture the beauty of travel and nature on these pages.

A handy color palette is included for each artwork, along with an example of my own finished artwork to guide you through every step of the way. Use these as inspiration, but don't feel limited – if you're drawn to different shades, follow your instincts and make each piece your own.

The numbers will help you get started as you build each artwork, color by color. It's a process, but it should also be enjoyable. Be playful, take your time, and don't worry too much about staying perfectly within the lines.

Before you begin, make sure you're sitting comfortably; work on a flat surface with your color selection laid out ready to go, a brush to hand, and a glass of water nearby for rinsing between shades. The paper in this book is 180gsm, so it is designed to work well with acrylics and watercolor paints.

You may want to let your artwork dry between colors to avoid smudging. It won't take long – just enough time to make a cup of tea, gaze out the window, or plan your next steps. Remember to always wash your brush thoroughly when changing colors to keep them clean and vibrant.

It's easy to lose yourself in painting, but do take a moment to stretch and adjust your posture when needed to stay comfortable.

Once your artwork is complete, use the cutting guides to cut it out and display it. Why not frame your favourite pieces and enjoy them in your home? Your creativity doesn't have to stay within the pages of this book.

Tools & materials

TOOLS, TEXTURES & TECHNIQUES

I work primarily with watercolor, but I also enjoy using gouache and acrylics. Watercolor has a beautiful unpredictability – the way the pigment flows across wet paper allows for both intentional marks and unexpected, expressive moments.

I often pair gouache with watercolor, using the two together to build depth and contrast. Gouache complements the softness of watercolor while adding richness, opacity, and vibrancy. For both, I use Winsor & Newton paints and typically work on either thick cartridge paper or hot-pressed watercolor paper.

When it comes to with acrylics, however, I tend to use them on their own. As a medium, they offer greater control and bold color, and I particularly enjoy how quickly they dry when building up layers. I use Derivan Matisse acrylics and usually paint on canvas.

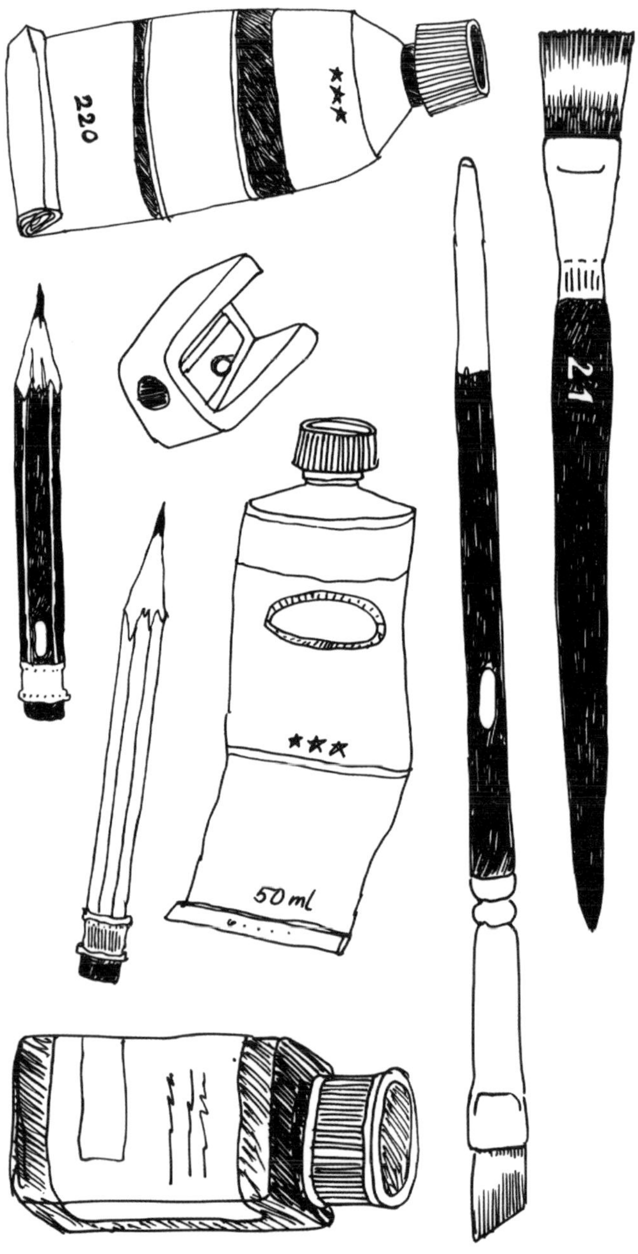

CARING FOR YOUR BRUSHES & MATERIALS

Looking after your brushes is essential – they're your most important tools, and you'll quickly find yourself favoring certain shapes and sizes.

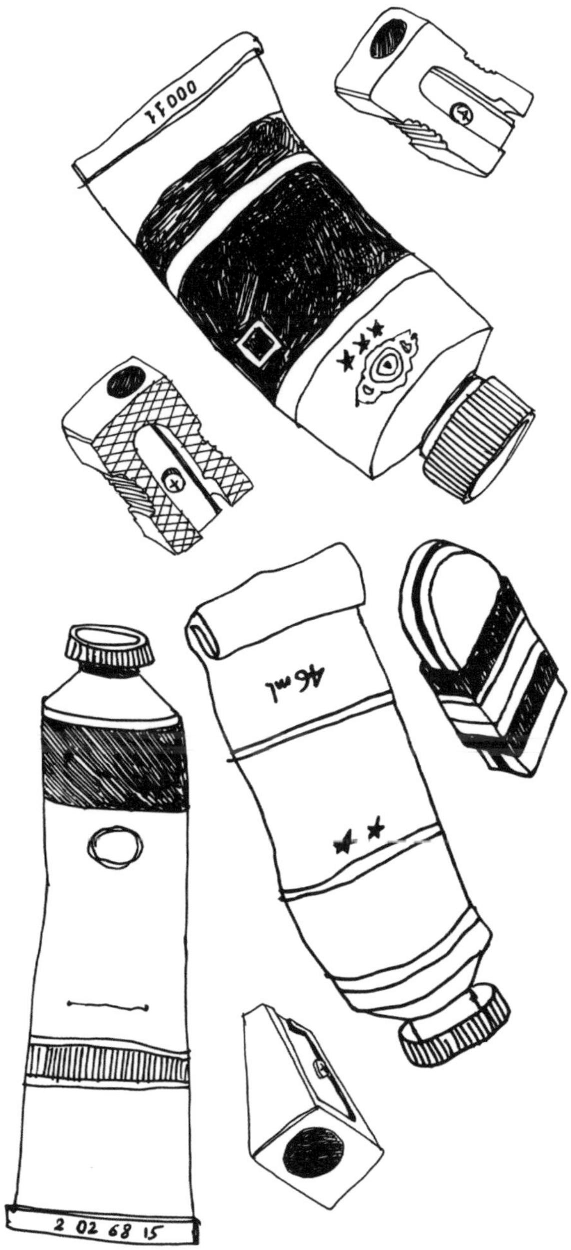

Always rinse them thoroughly after each session, and never leave them standing bristle-down in water, as this can bend and damage their shape over time. Gently reshape the bristles and leave them to dry flat or upright.

For acrylic painting in particular, keep a water spray nearby to prevent your paints from drying out on the palette. A stay-wet palette is also a worthwhile investment if you work with acrylics regularly – especially useful when working on paint-by-numbers pieces, as it keeps your colors fresh and consistent throughout.

GETTING STARTED: KEEP IT SIMPLE

My biggest piece of advice is not to overwhelm yourself at the beginning – you really don't need much to get started.

For watercolors, a small set of good-quality paints, a couple of reliable brushes (a round brush in two sizes will take you a long way).

For acrylics, begin with a few key colors and experiment with mixing. Working within a limited palette is not only practical, but also a great creative exercise – you might be surprised by how much you can achieve with just a handful of shades.

Finding your creativity

FINDING YOUR COLOR PALETTE

Color inspiration can come from anywhere, and I truly believe everyone has a palette they're naturally drawn to. I tend to gravitate towards warmer tones like pinks, warm greens, and yellows, rather than cooler blues and purples.

That said, it's always worth experimenting. I regularly save color combinations that catch my eye, whether from photographs, fabrics, or even a beautifully presented meal.

I'd encourage you to start your own color inspiration folder - or a Pinterest board - and return to it whenever you sit down to paint. It's a simple way to build confidence and develop your personal style.

The palette provided in this book offers a glimpse into how I approach color. Think of it as a starting point - one that, with time, will help you create and refine palettes that are entirely your own.

FINDING INSPIRATION

I'm often most inspired when I'm traveling - discovering new landscapes and experiencing different cultures have always sparked some of my best ideas.

That said, inspiration is everywhere once you start to notice it. Even on quieter days, when I haven't gone far and feel creatively flat, simply sitting down and putting paint to paper can unlock something unexpected.

That's part of the beauty of paint by numbers - it removes the pressure of the blank canvas and lets you focus on the simple enjoyment of painting. Sometimes a little structure is exactly what you need to find your flow.

EXPLORING COLOR WITH CONFIDENCE

Don't be afraid to experiment - some of the most interesting results come from trying something new. A helpful starting point is a basic understanding of color theory: warm and cool tones, how complementary colors create contrast and energy, and how analogous colors bring a sense of harmony.

If you ever feel stuck, turn to nature. A landscape or garden can be a perfect source of inspiration - try picking out five colors you can see and use them as the foundation for your palette.

It can also help to limit the number of colors you use. Working within a smaller palette prevents overcomplication and often leads to more thoughtful results. And remember, white space and neutrals can be just as impactful as bold, vibrant color.

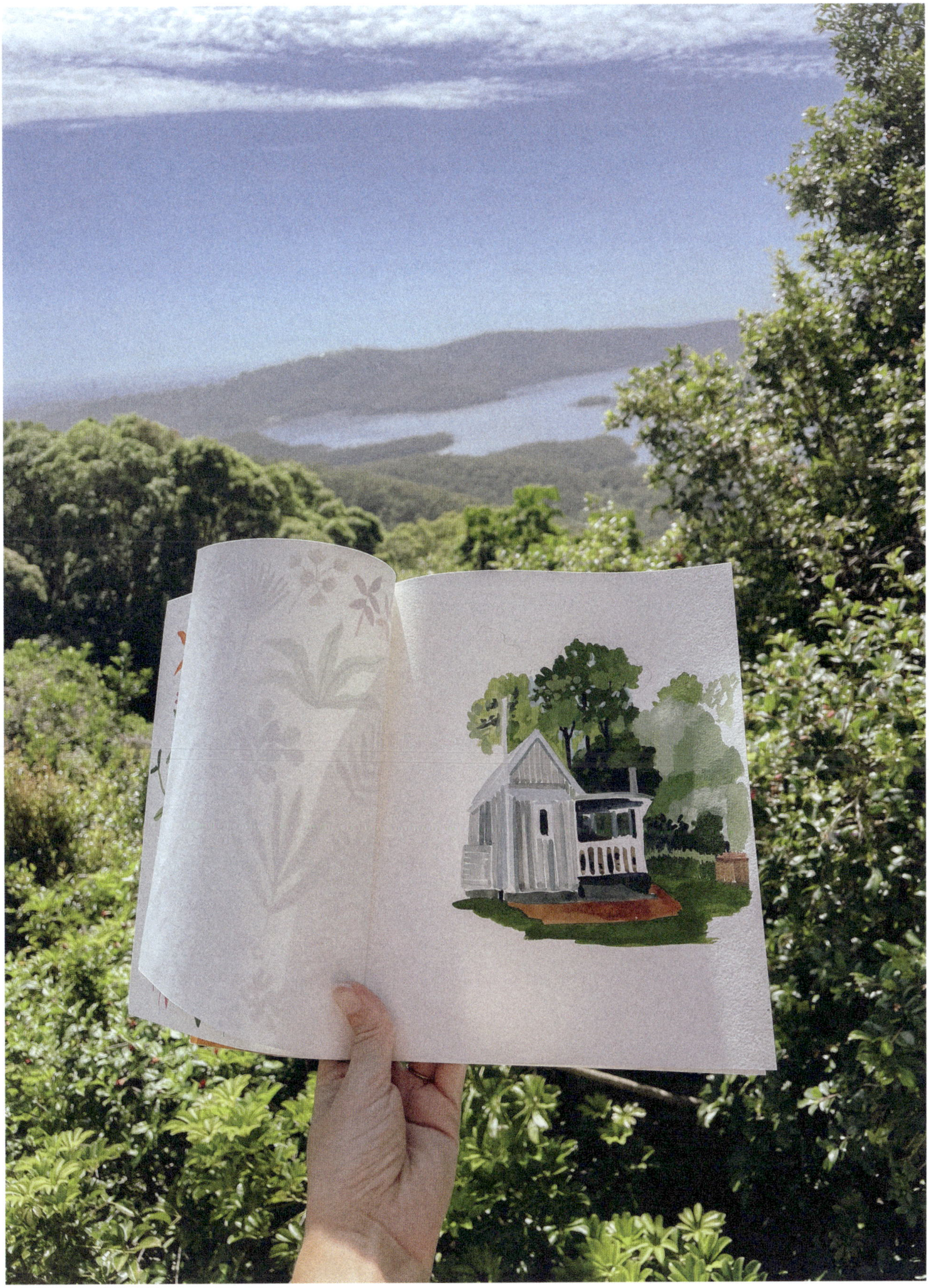

THE DOLOMITES, ITALY

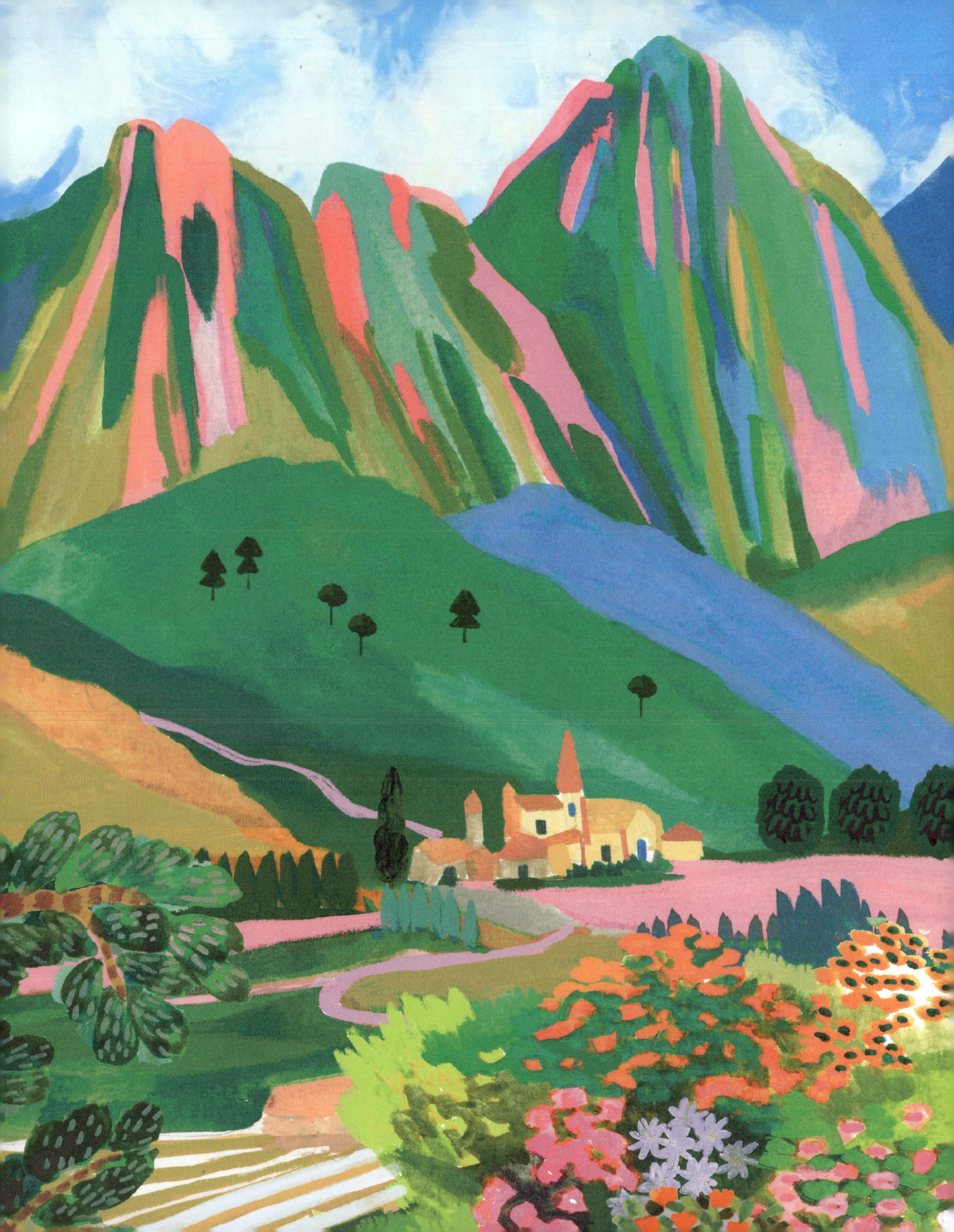

The Dolomites, Italy

Particularly rugged mountains that stretch sharply up towards the sky, the Dolomites combine sheer peaks with valleys and alpine meadows that help to hide some especially magical villages. This north-eastern region of Italy is a paradise for hikers, cyclists, skiers, climbers, naturalists, oenophiles, gastronomes and artists alike!

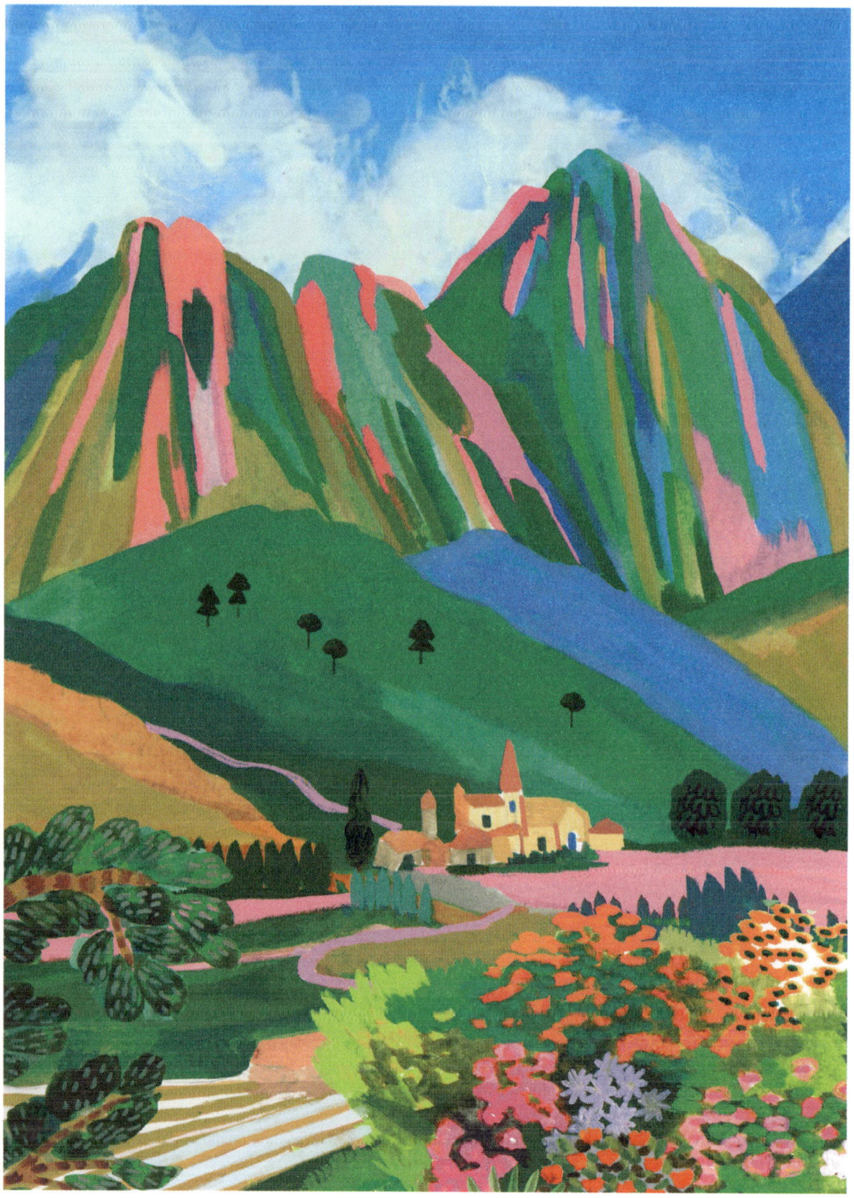

STEP BY STEP

- Start with the blue of the sky
- Then fill in the bigger expanses of blue, green and pink
- Next, fill in the streaks of blues, greens and pinks
- Finish with the village, flowers and trees

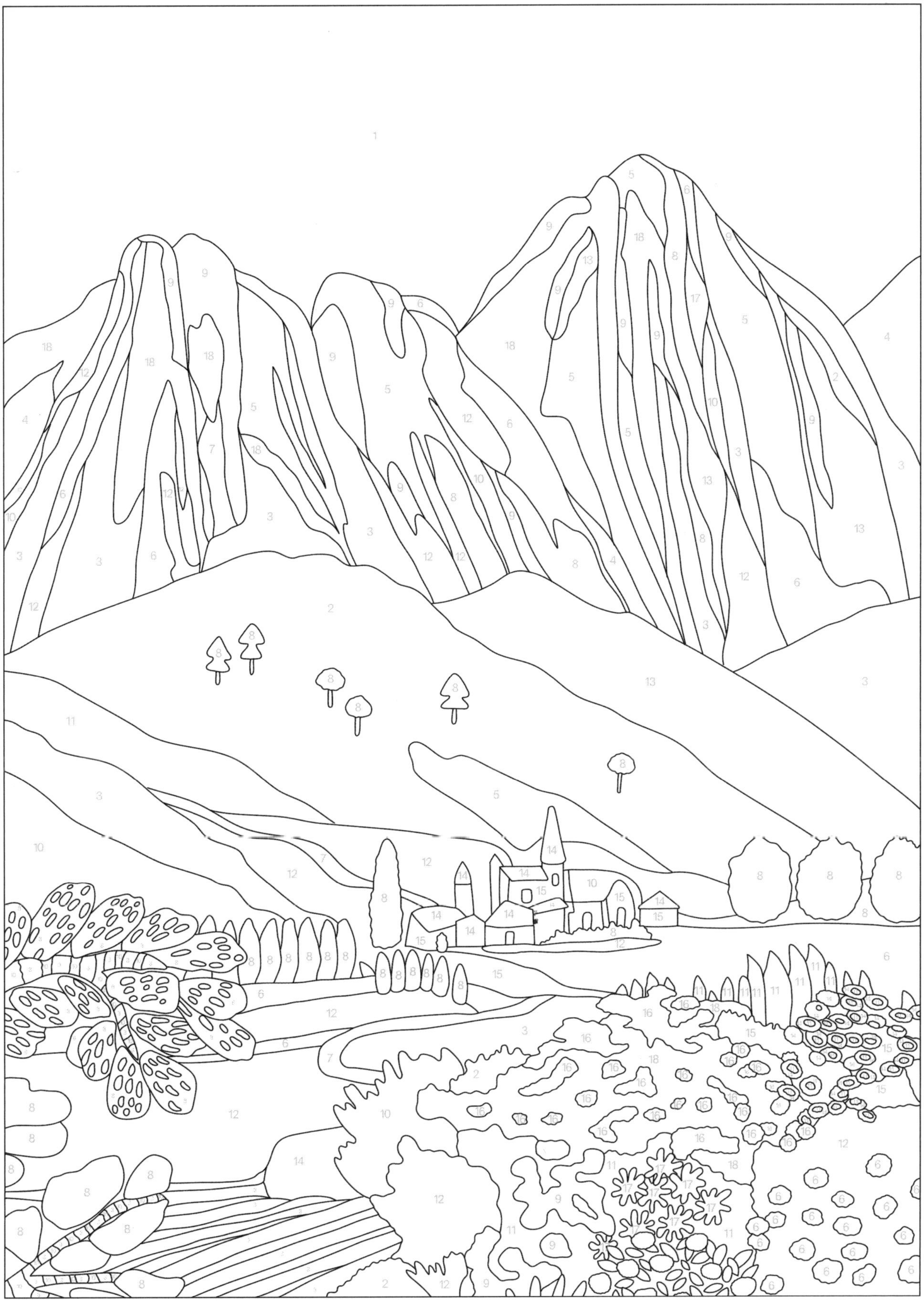

AMALFI SUNSET, ITALY

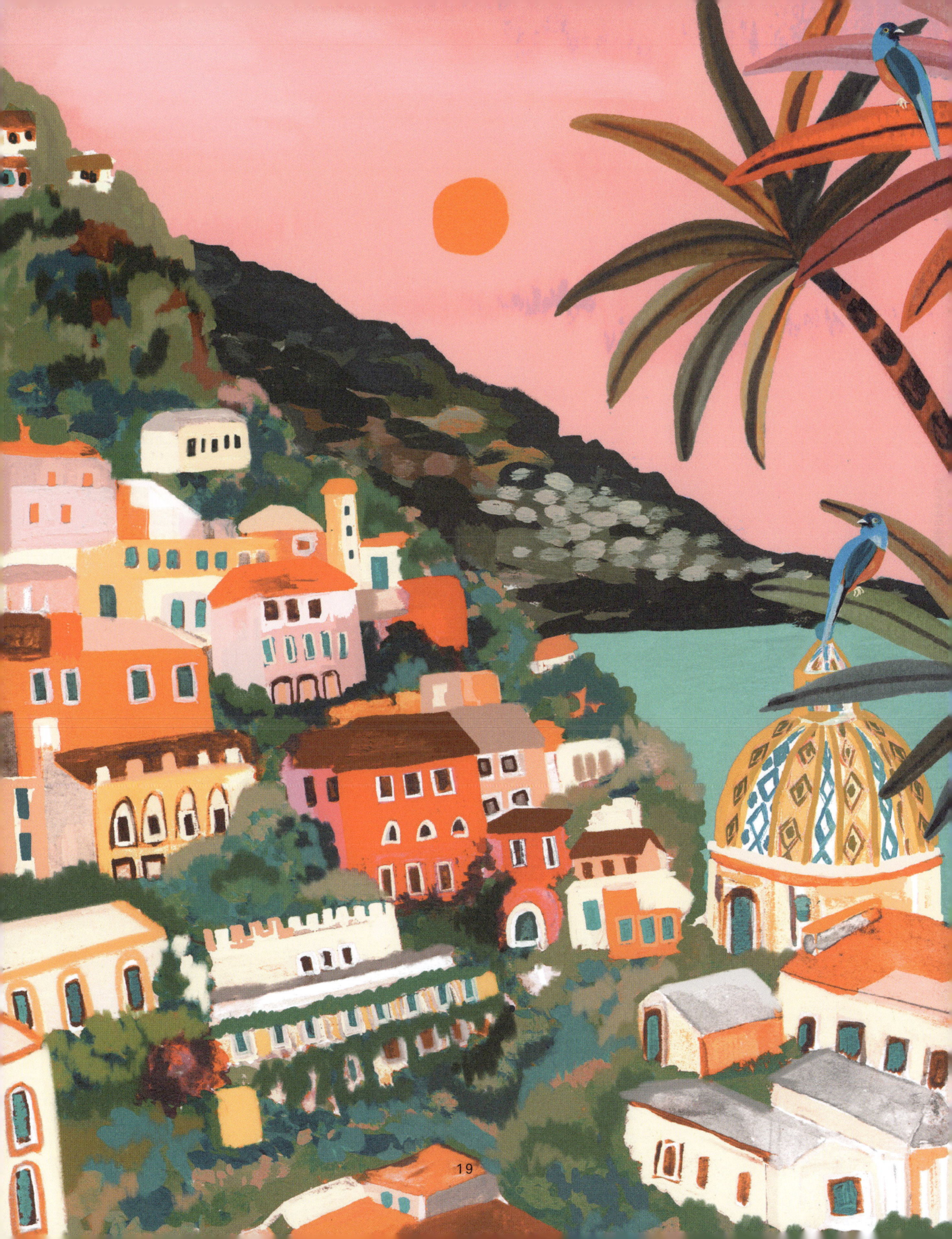

Amalfi Sunset, Italy

Amalfi is a UNESCO World Heritage Site and a contender for the most beautiful place in Italy. Combining cliffs, coast and color, it's a must-see resort full of stunning beaches, teetering cliff-side bars, and world-famous lemons. Visit Amalfi for the culture, hiking and food; stay for the painterly sunsets and celebrity-spotting.

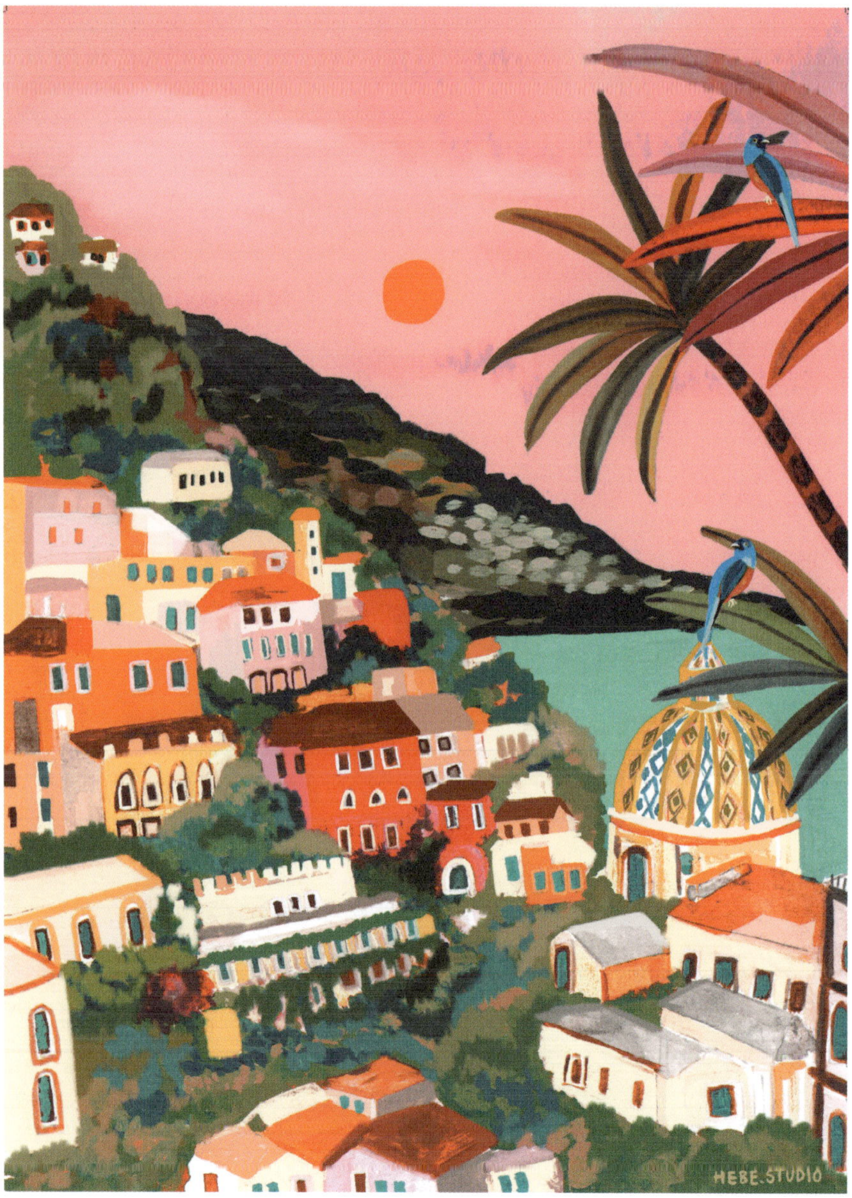

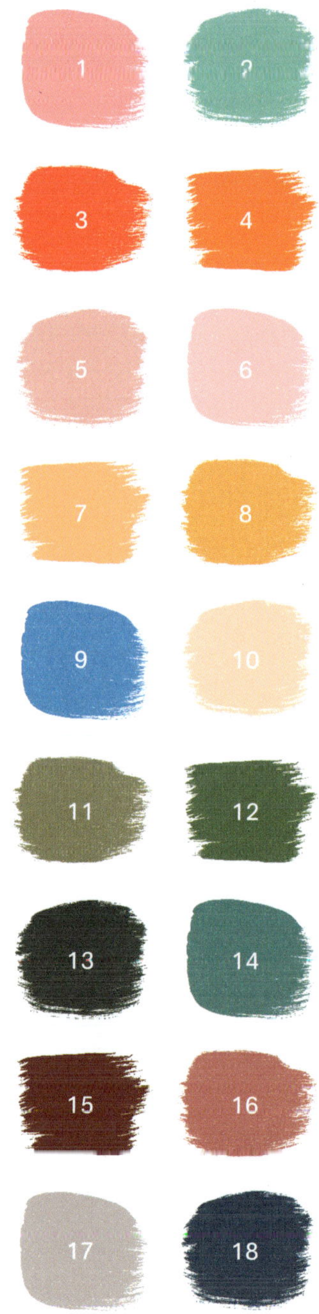

STEP BY STEP

- Start with the pink sky and blue sea
- Now fill in the buildings
- Add in the shades of green dotted around the cliffs
- Finish with the windows, sun and other details

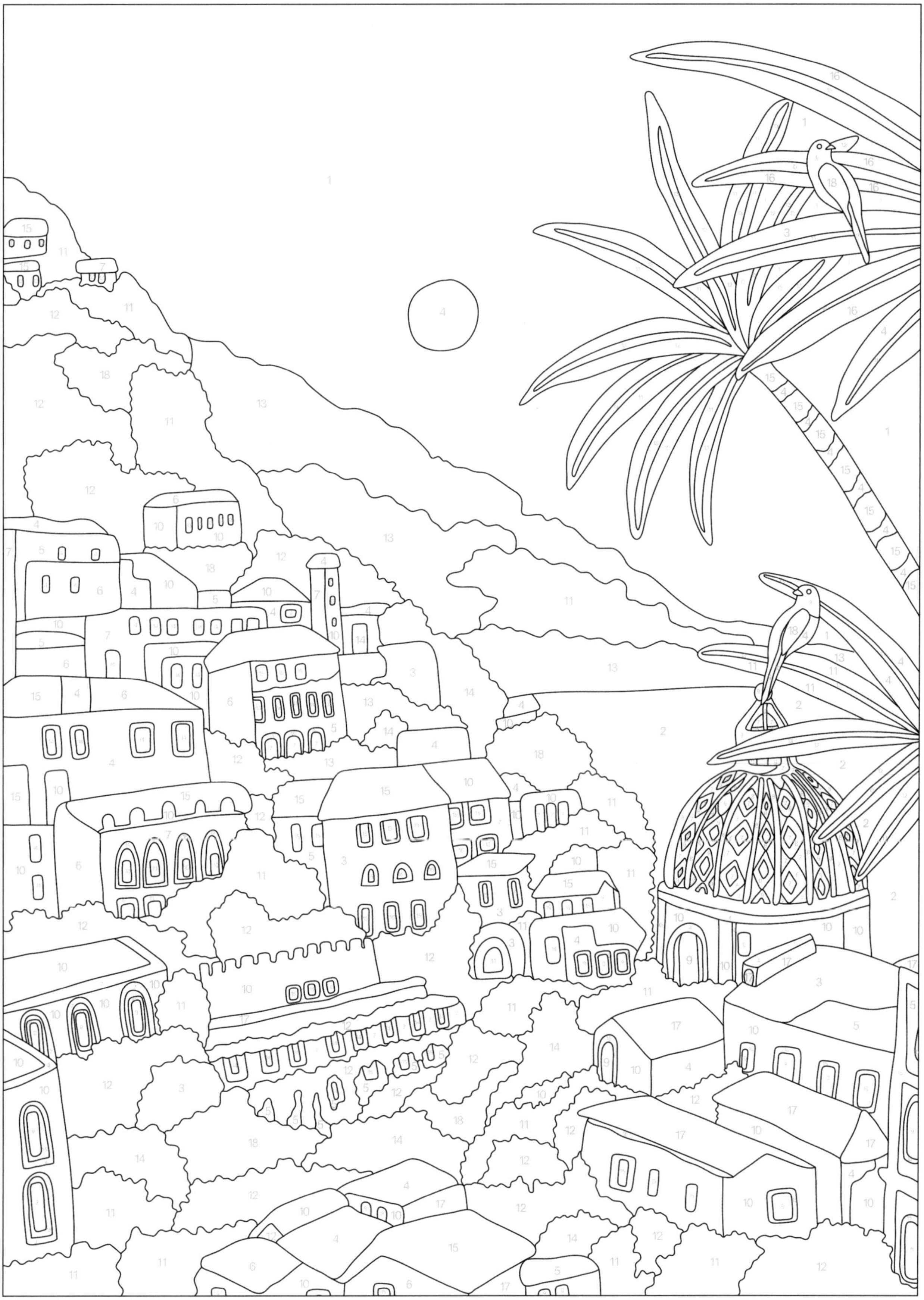

CAPPADOCIA, TURKEY

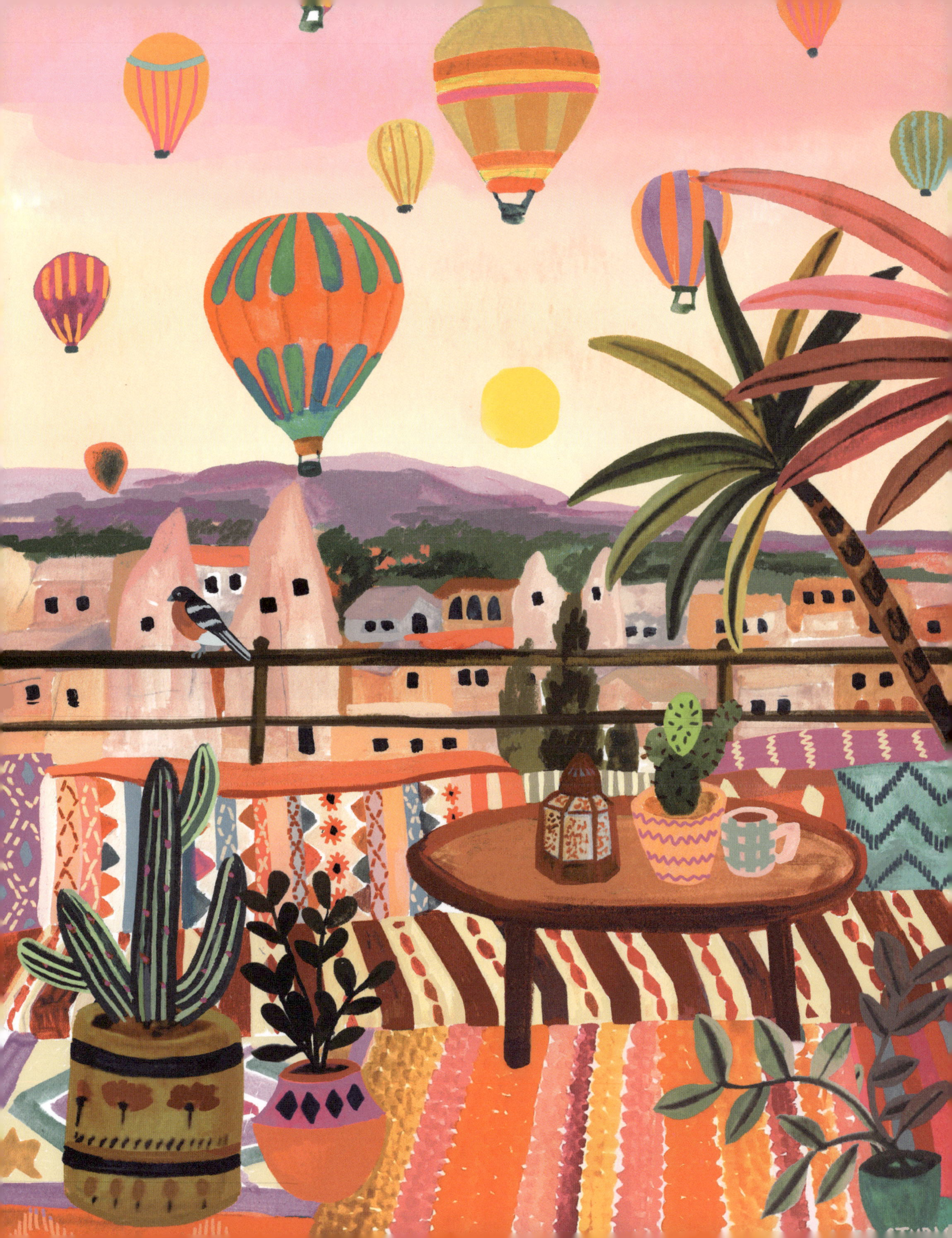

Cappadocia, Turkey

It's hard to imagine a more generous sensory experience than a visit to Cappodocia in Turkey. The rewards are many and none more so than the sights: the moonscapes – geological features known as 'fairy chimneys' and cave dwellings – the opulent textiles, the hot air balloons filling the sky at sunrise, the horses for which the region is famous. There's so much to see and recollect, one detail at a time.

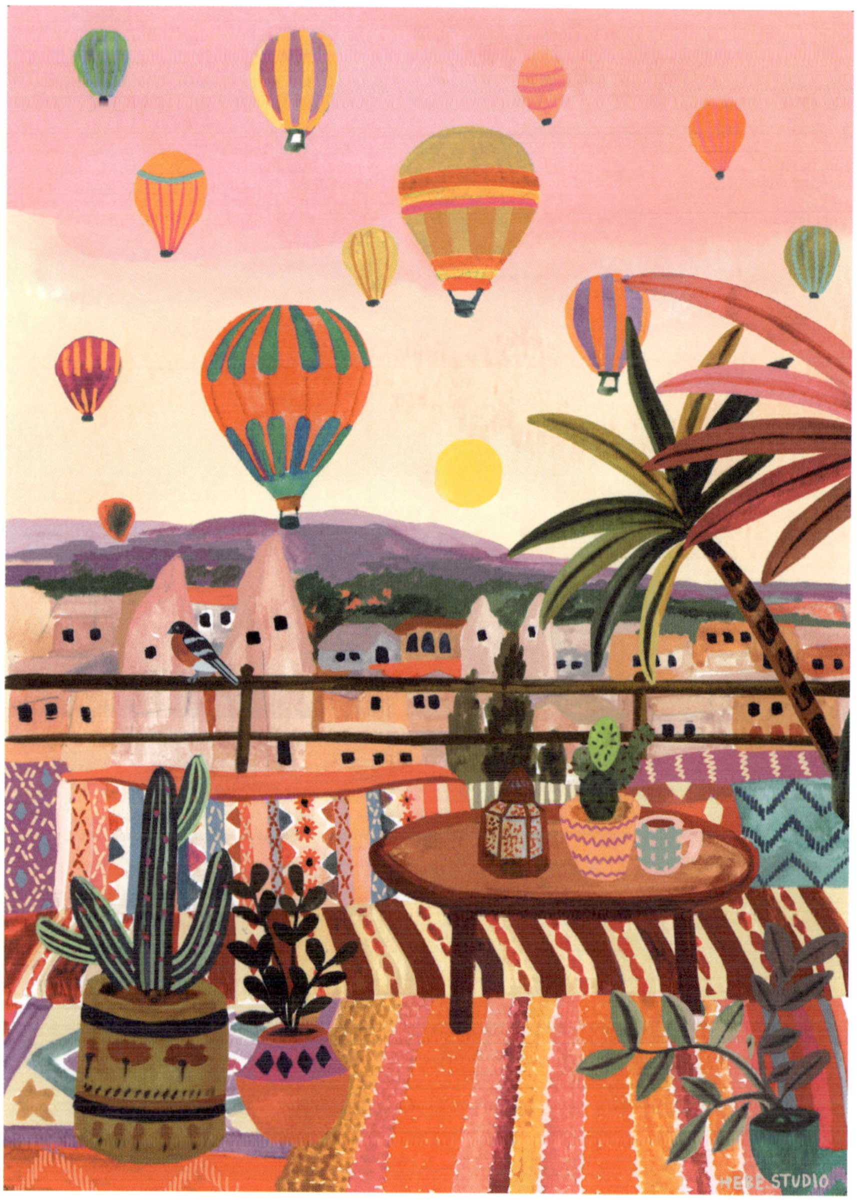

STEP BY STEP

- Start with the pink and orange of the sky
- Move on to the orangey buildings
- Take your time over the details of the balcony furnishings
- Finish with the balloons, plants and little windows

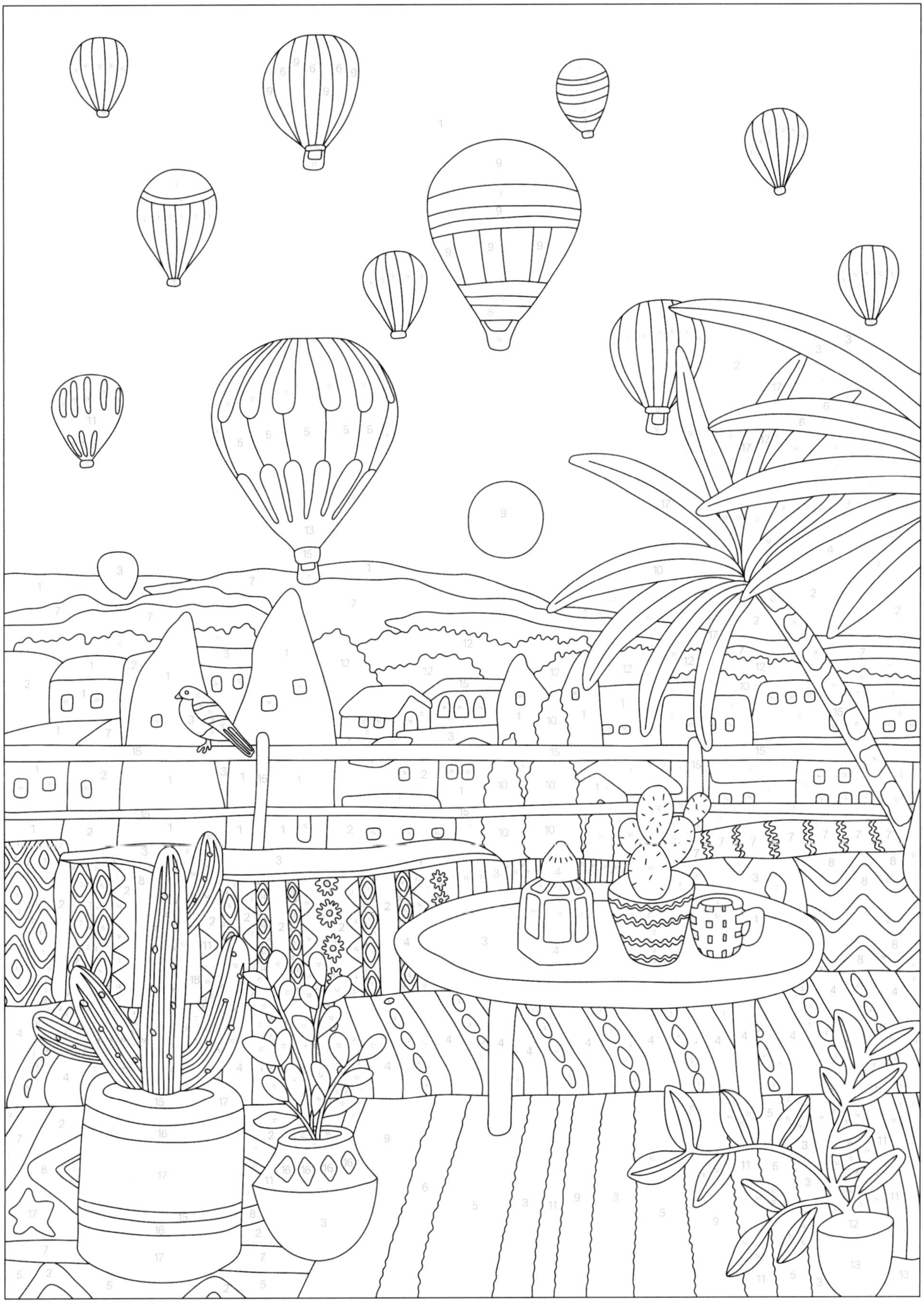

SAKURA TREES, JAPAN

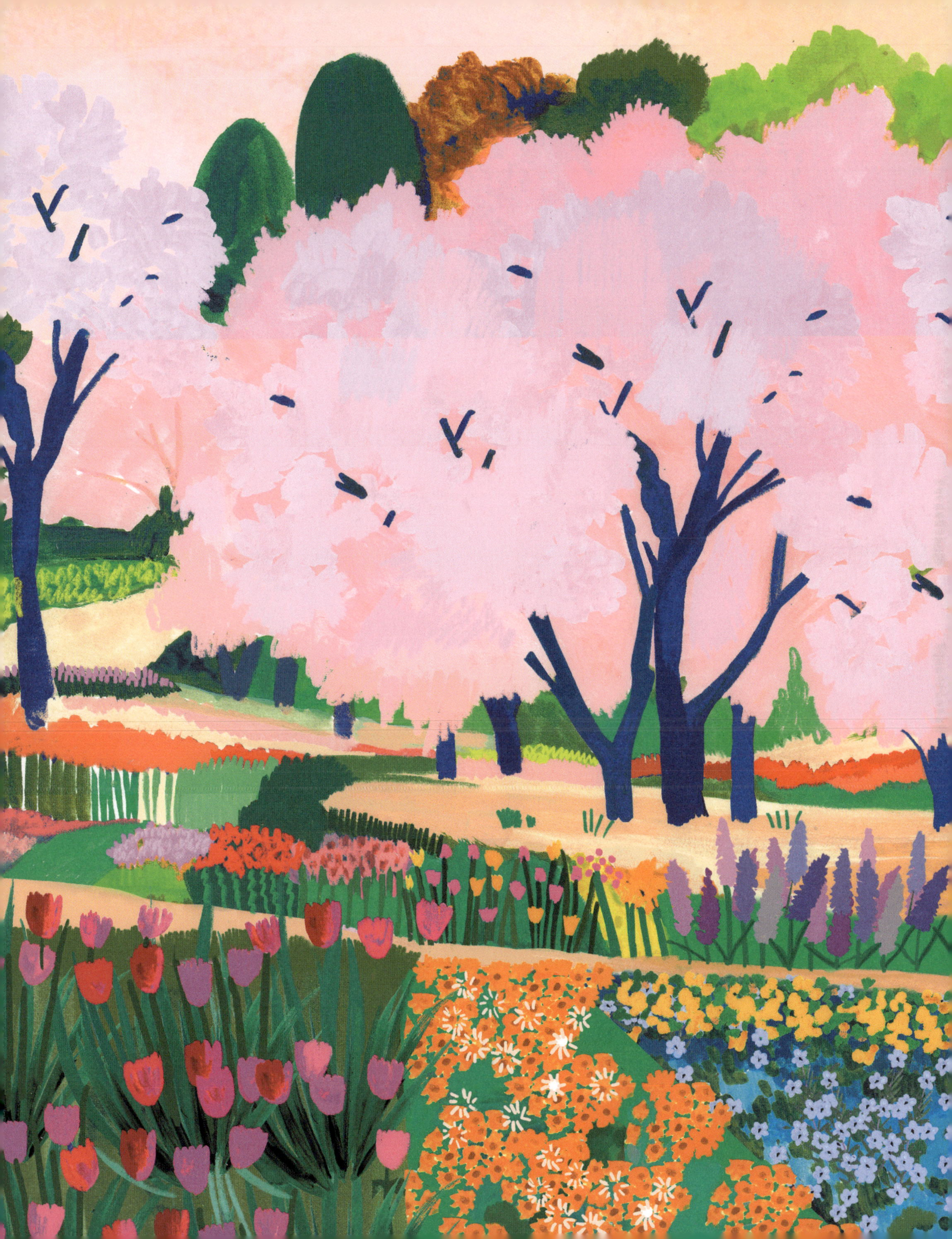

Sakura Trees, Japan

Cherry blossom – 'sakura' – is the ultimate expression of spring, lining streets with cloud-like trees and carpeting the ground with delicate pink flowers. The spiritual home of sakura is Japan, where people flock to the best sakura spots and take part in 'flower-viewing' parties called 'hanami'. So cherished are these trees in bloom that Japanese riends and colleagues often visit nearby parks to sit and picnic under the beautiful trees.

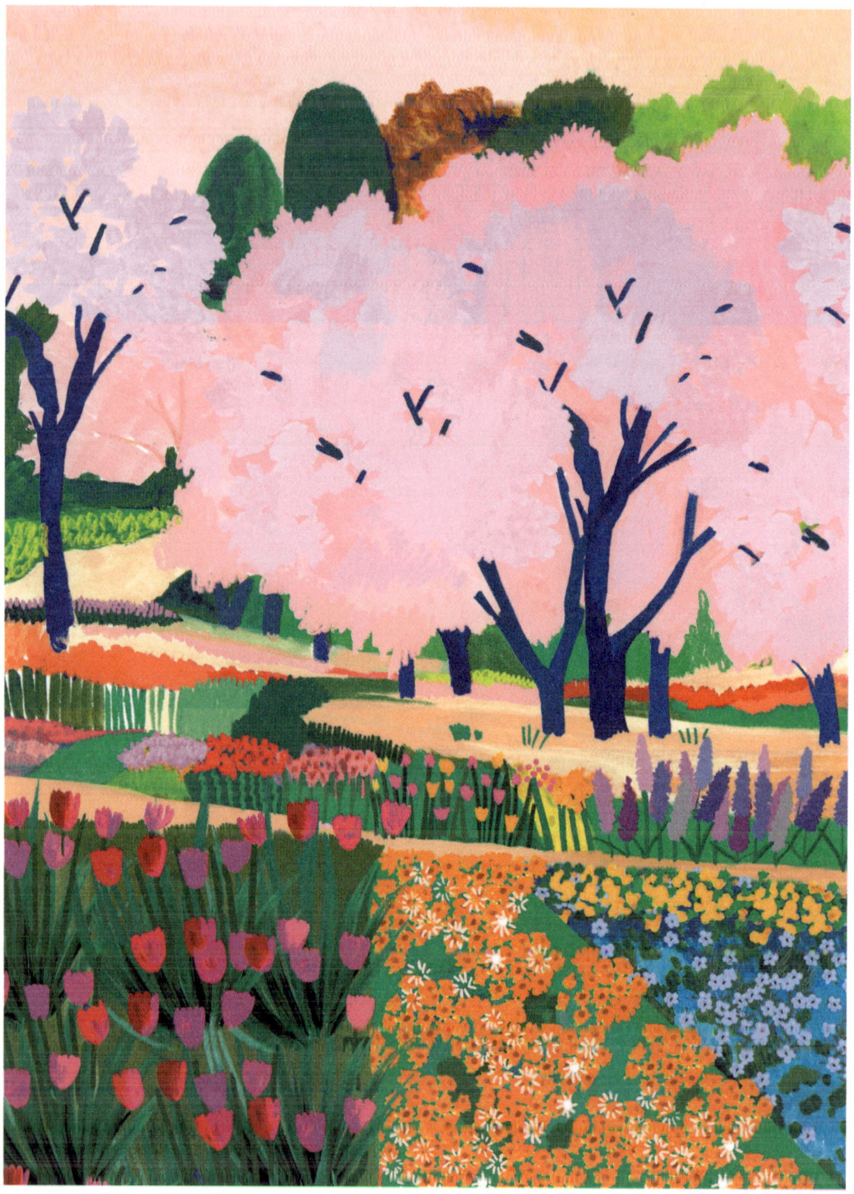

STEP BY STEP

- Start with the peach sky
- Now do the pink cherry blossom
- Fill in the greens of the trees and plants
- Finish with the many flowers and other details

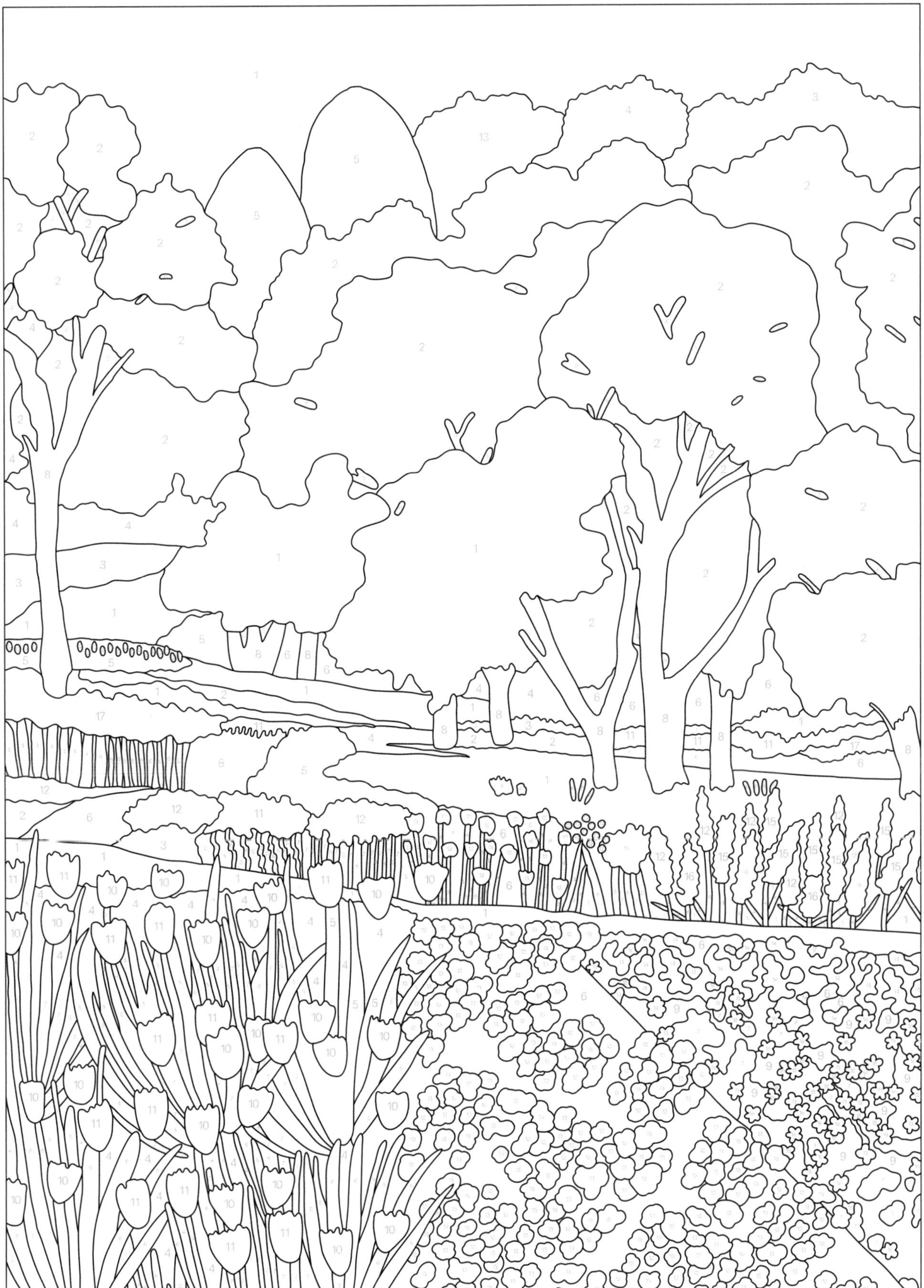

LAKE TEKAPO, NEW ZEALAND

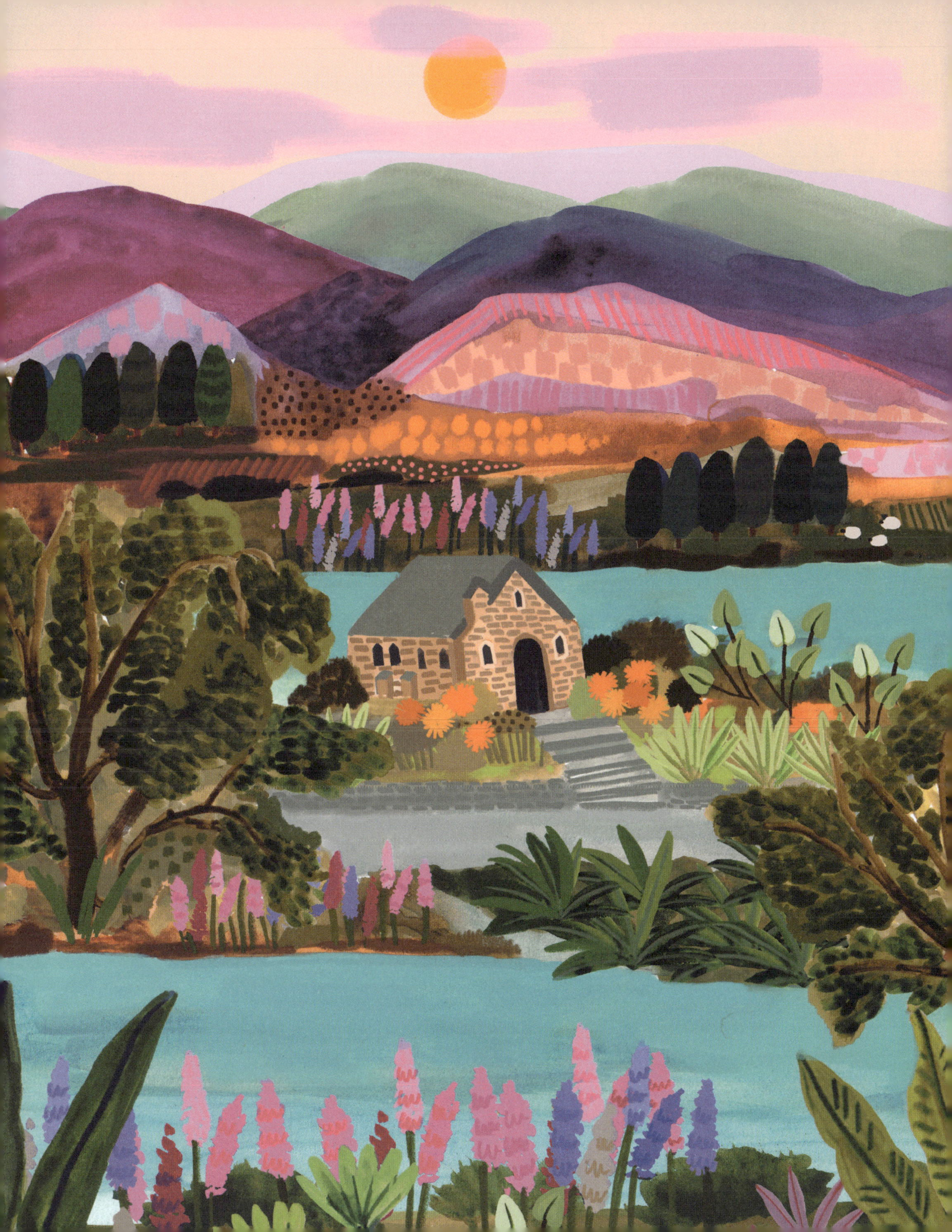

Lake Tekapo, New Zealand

Celebrated for its turquoise water, Lake Tekapo is a place of dazzling wonder. The Church of the Good Shepherd, right on the shore of the lake, was built in honor of the magnificence of the setting. Everything around the lake enhances this iconic place – the vivid lupins, the hot pools, the world-class night-time stargazing, the surrounding mountains. It's a haven, complete with a vibrant color palette.

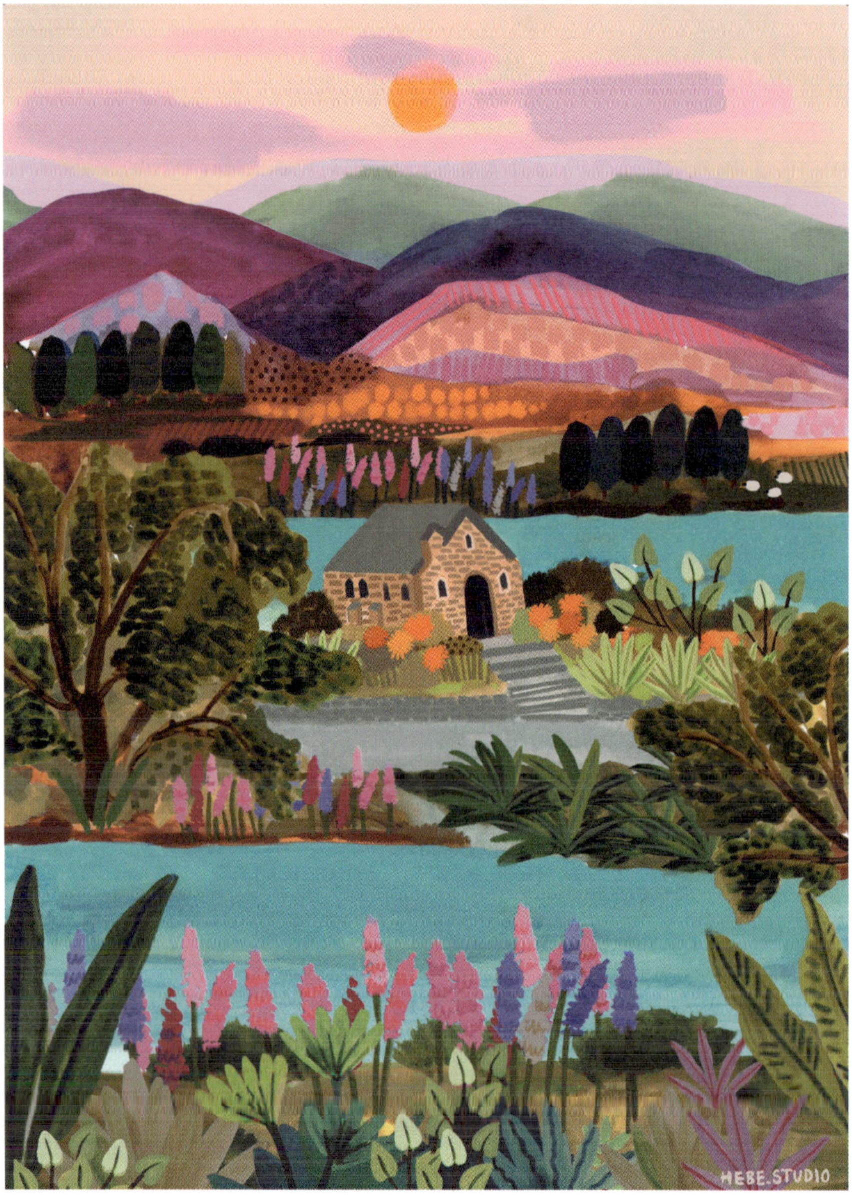

STEP BY STEP

- Start with the pink of the sky
- Add the blue water
- Move on to the purples and pinks of the mountains
- Finish with the vegetation and the church

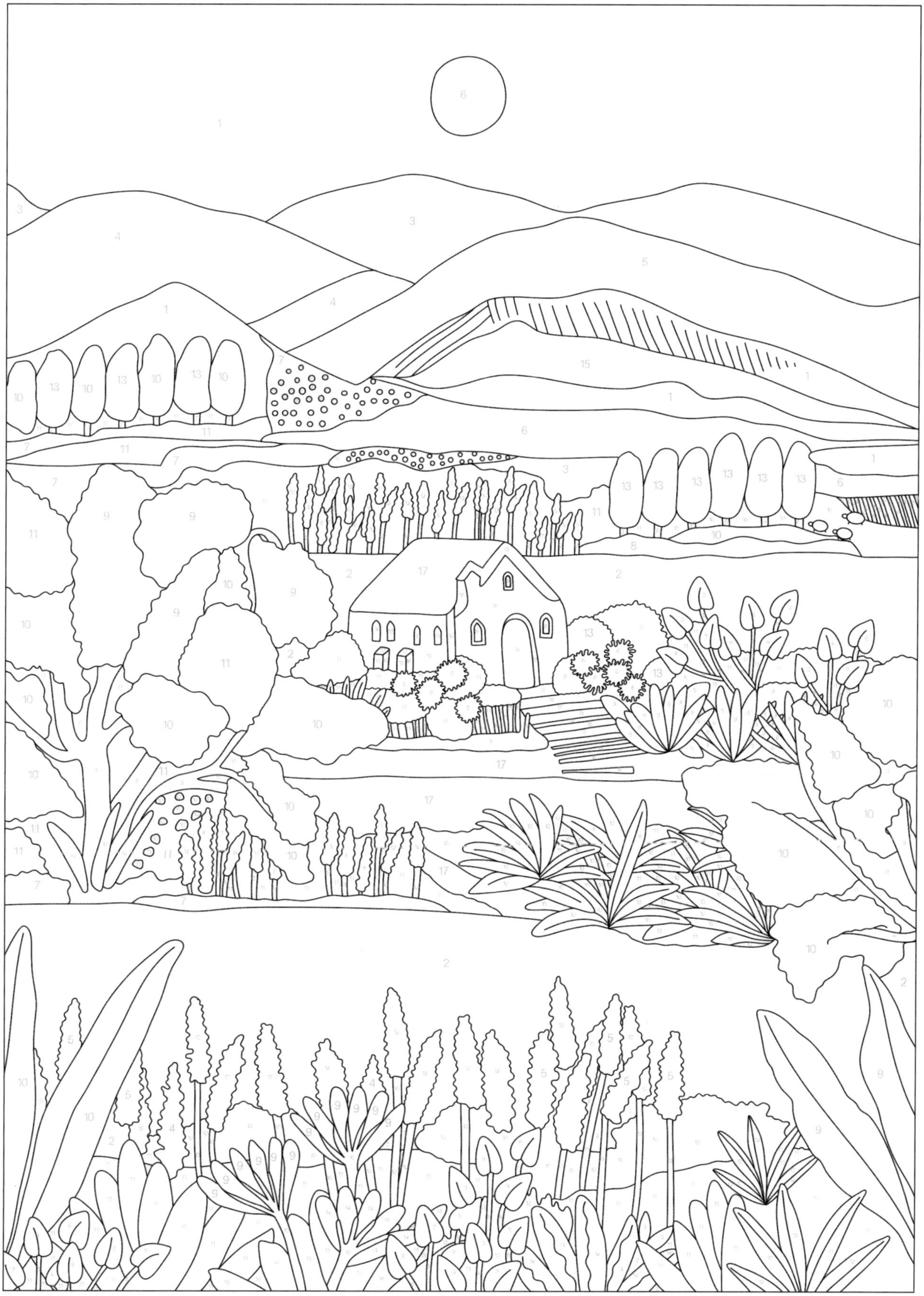

LOTUS GATE, INDIA

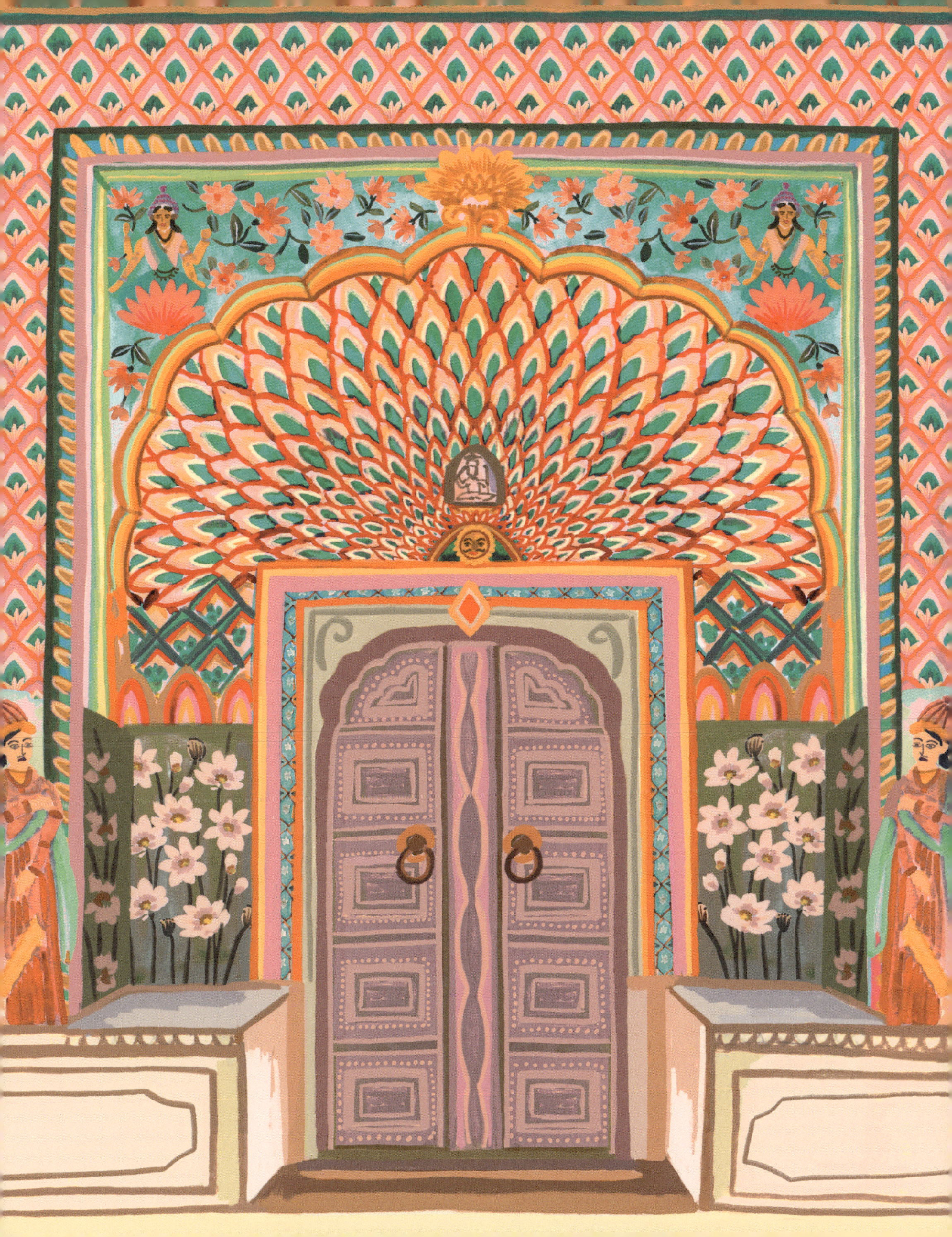

Lotus Gate, India

Immerse yourself in this symbol of summer – the Lotus Gate and archway from the City Palace in Jaipur, commonly known as the Pink City. Think of yourself standing in front of the gate, applying each delicate touch of color, starting with the tiniest petals and strokes, and building outwards to create the effect of a peacock in a summer garden of lotus flowers… Heavenly.

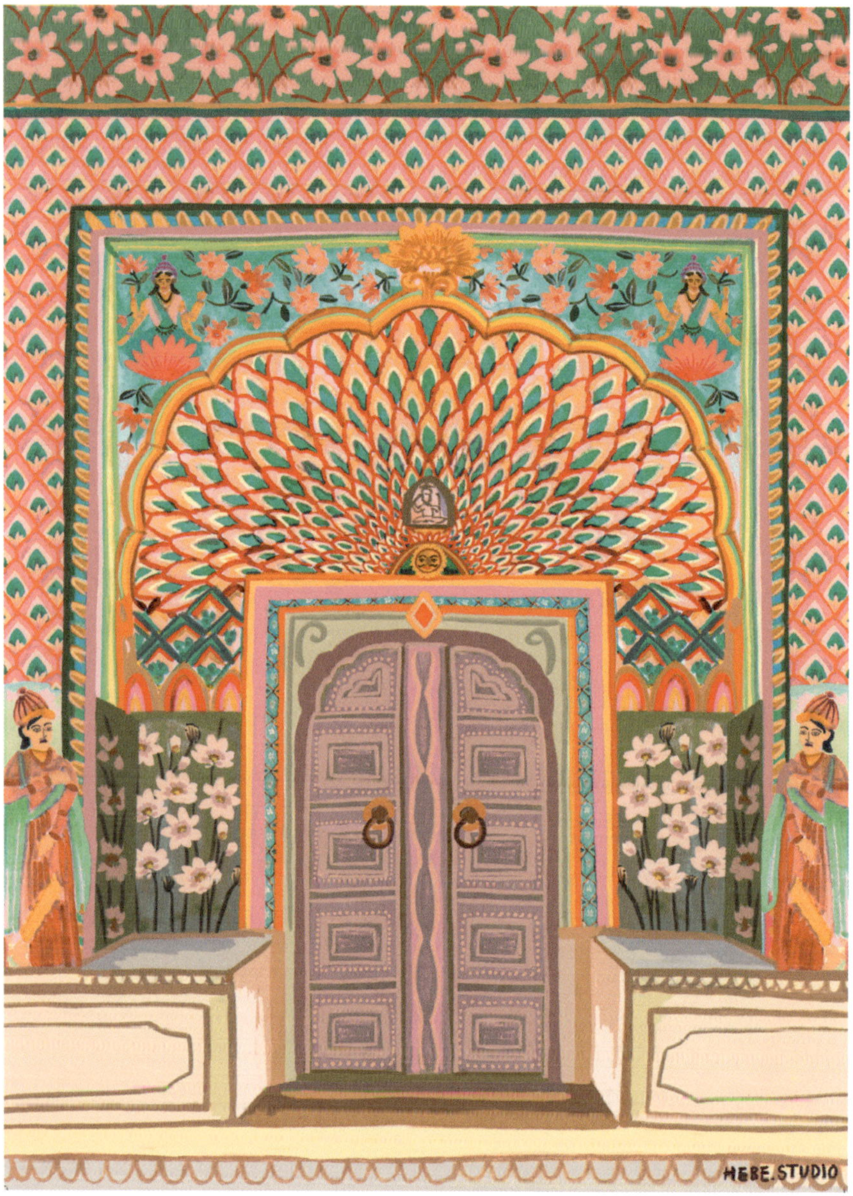

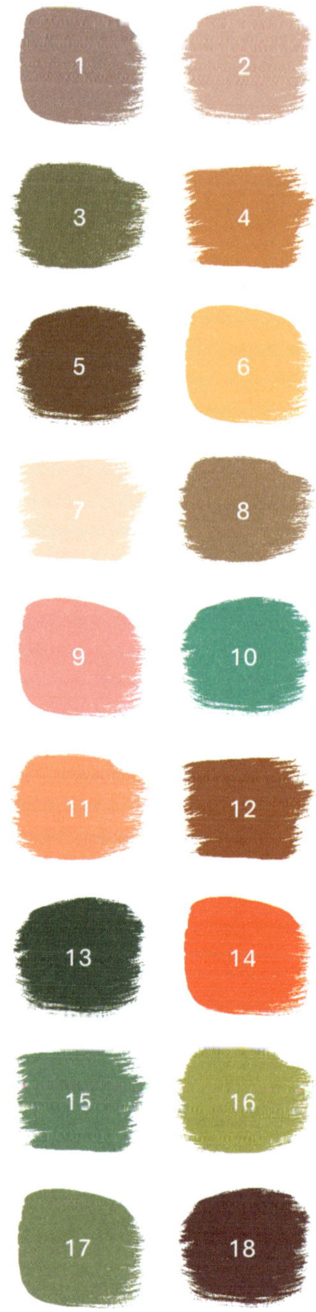

STEP BY STEP

- Start with the door and simpler patches of color in the foreground
- Move on to the background greens beside and above the door
- Tackle the figures on the left and right of the picture
- Fill in all the finer details, flowers and shapes

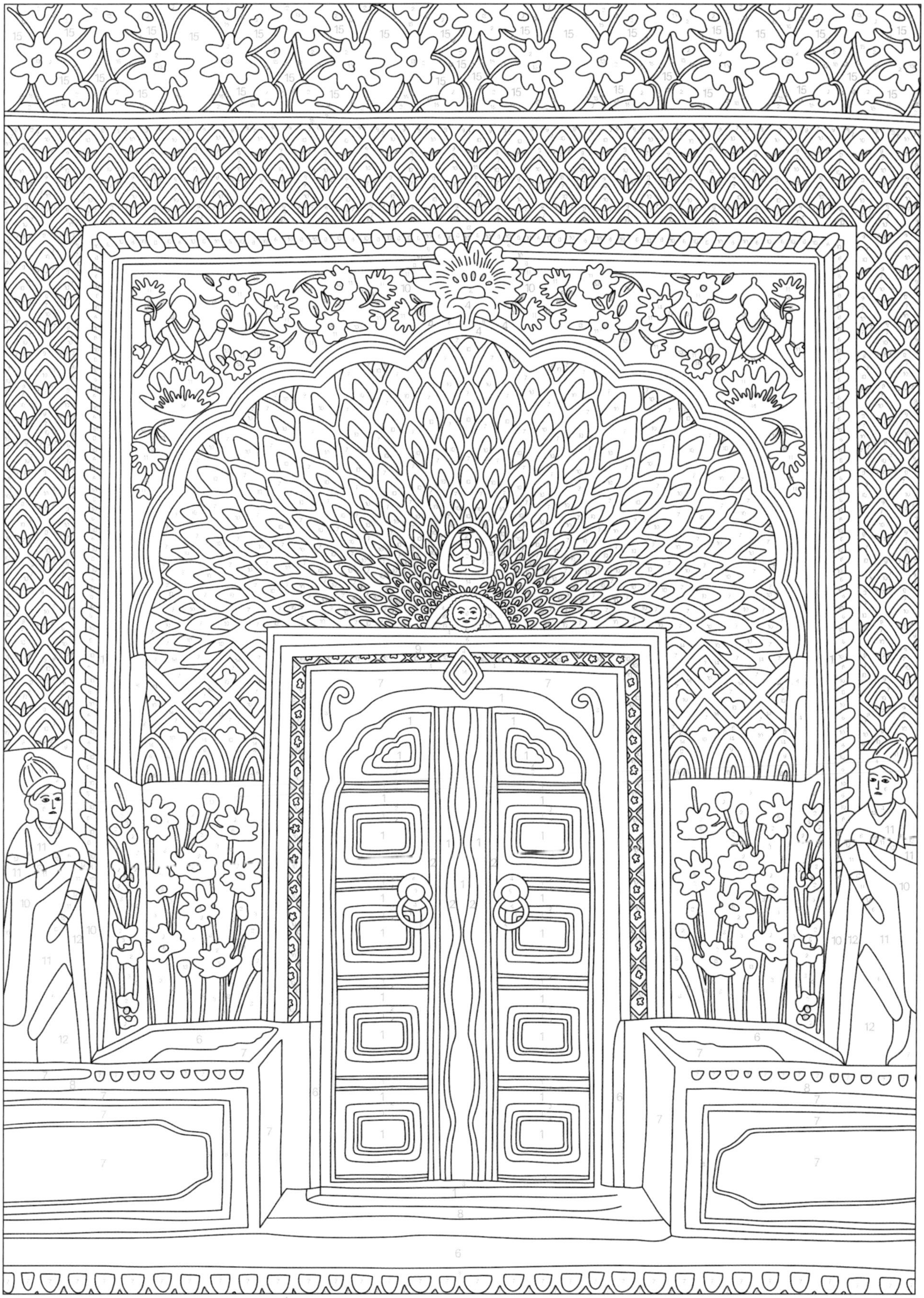

ELLA,
SRI LANKA

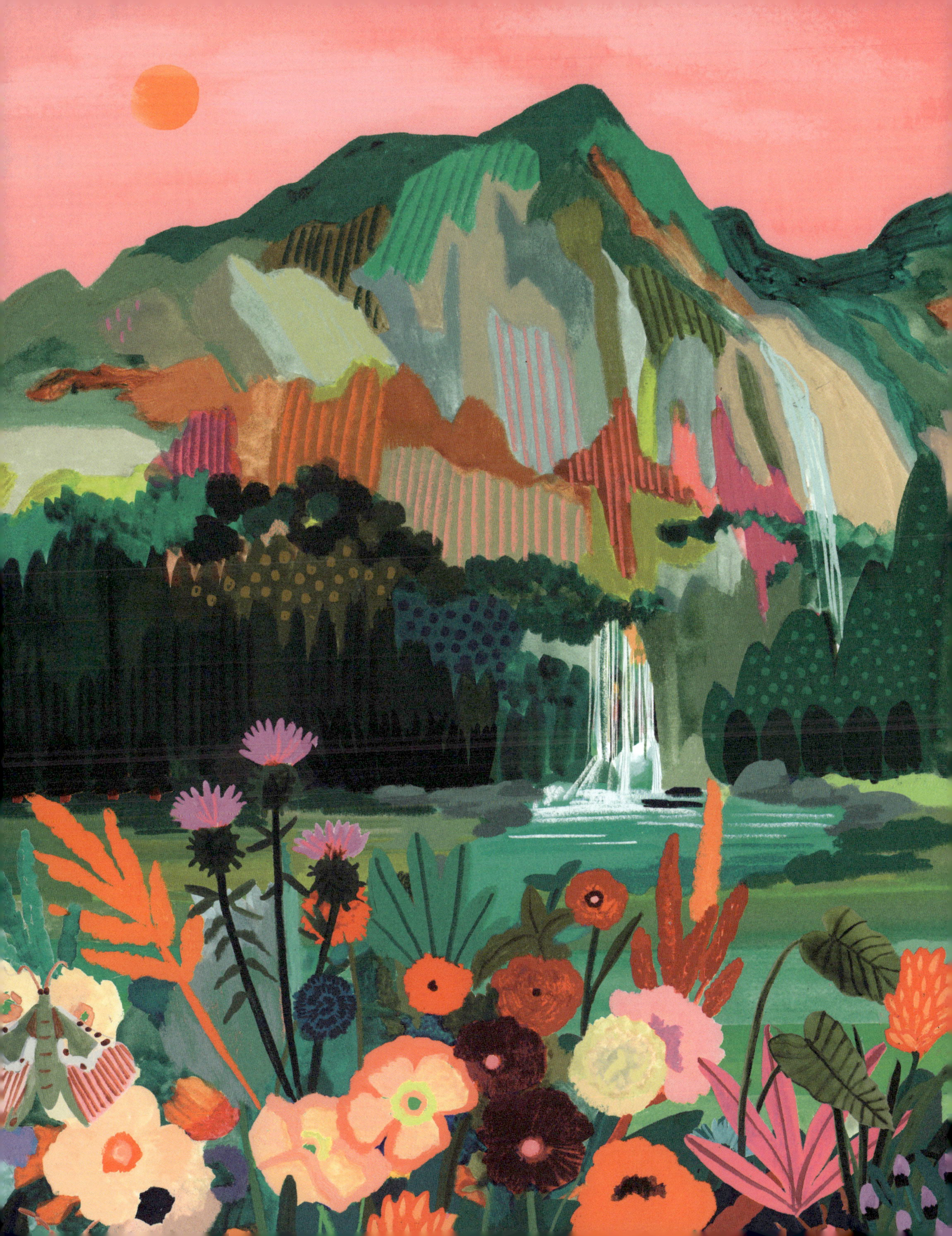

Ella, Sri Lanka

Transport yourself to a mountain village in Sri Lanka where the view is of tea plantations, lush greenery and waterfalls, and the air is of the purest quality. It's not quite time for the breathtaking train ride over the railway bridge all the way to Kandy, so you sit and admire the scenery for a while instead. As you work your way through all the colors you can see, you experience an immense feeling of peace.

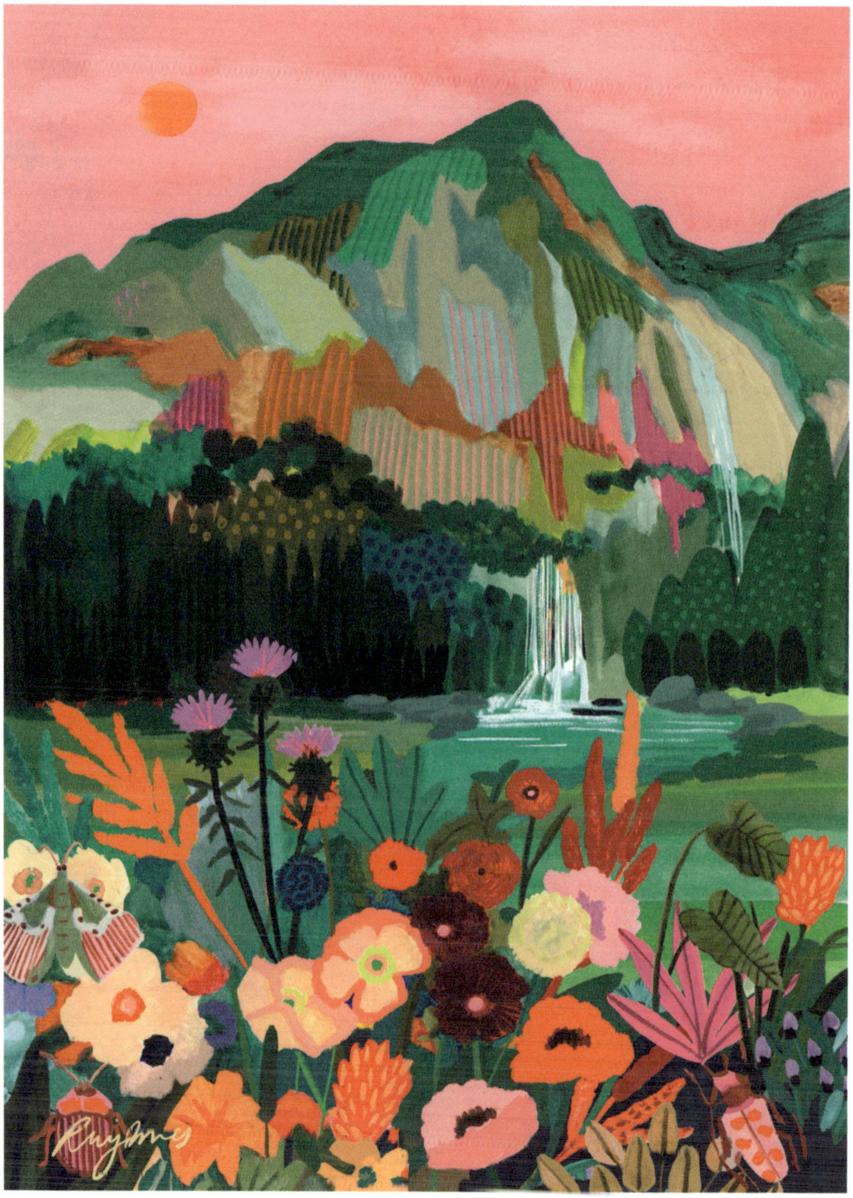

STEP BY STEP

- Start with the pink sky
- Apply the different textures of green
- Add the non-green parts of the mountain
- Finish with the flowers, waterfall and sun

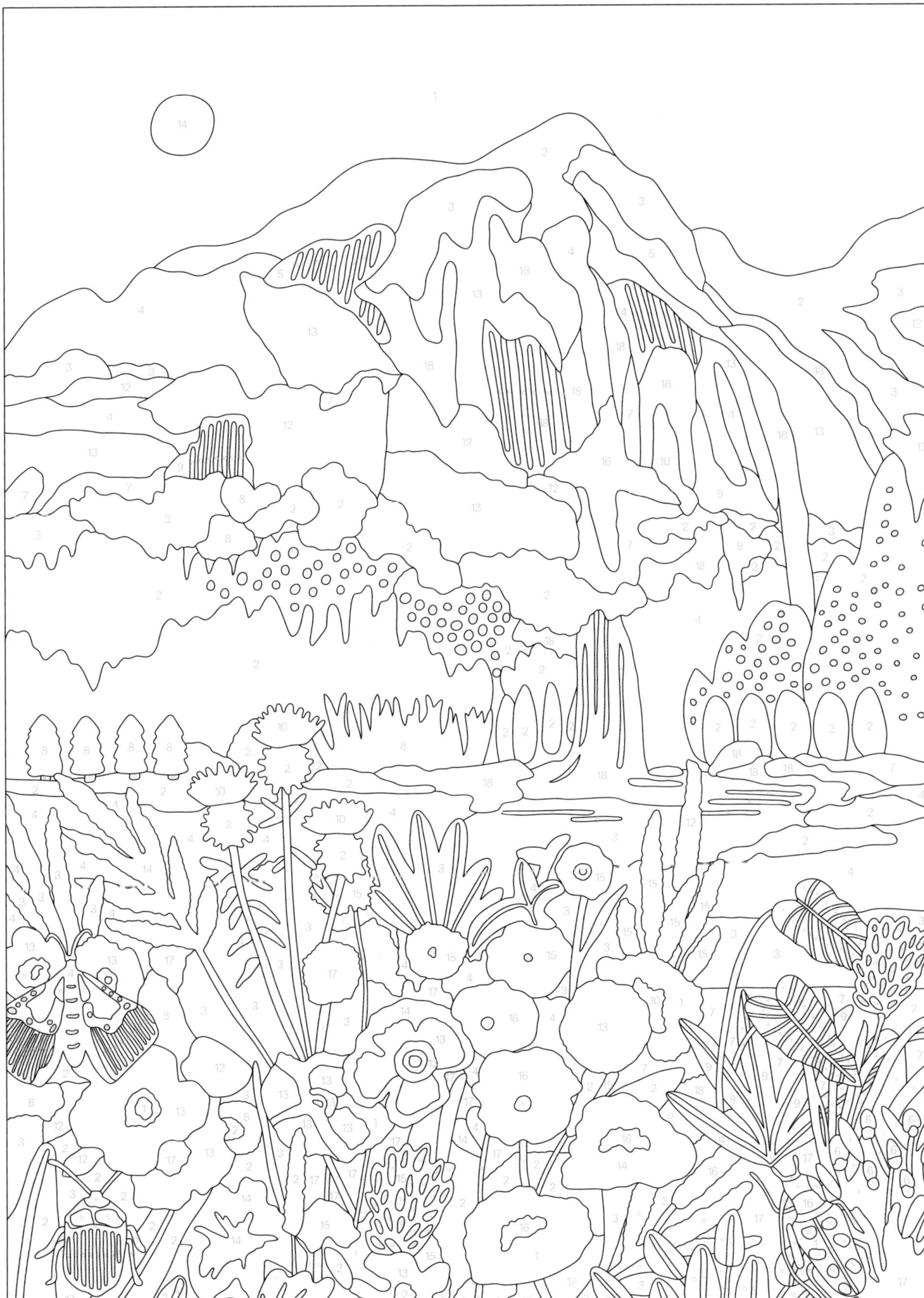

TRAIN RIDE IN JAPAN

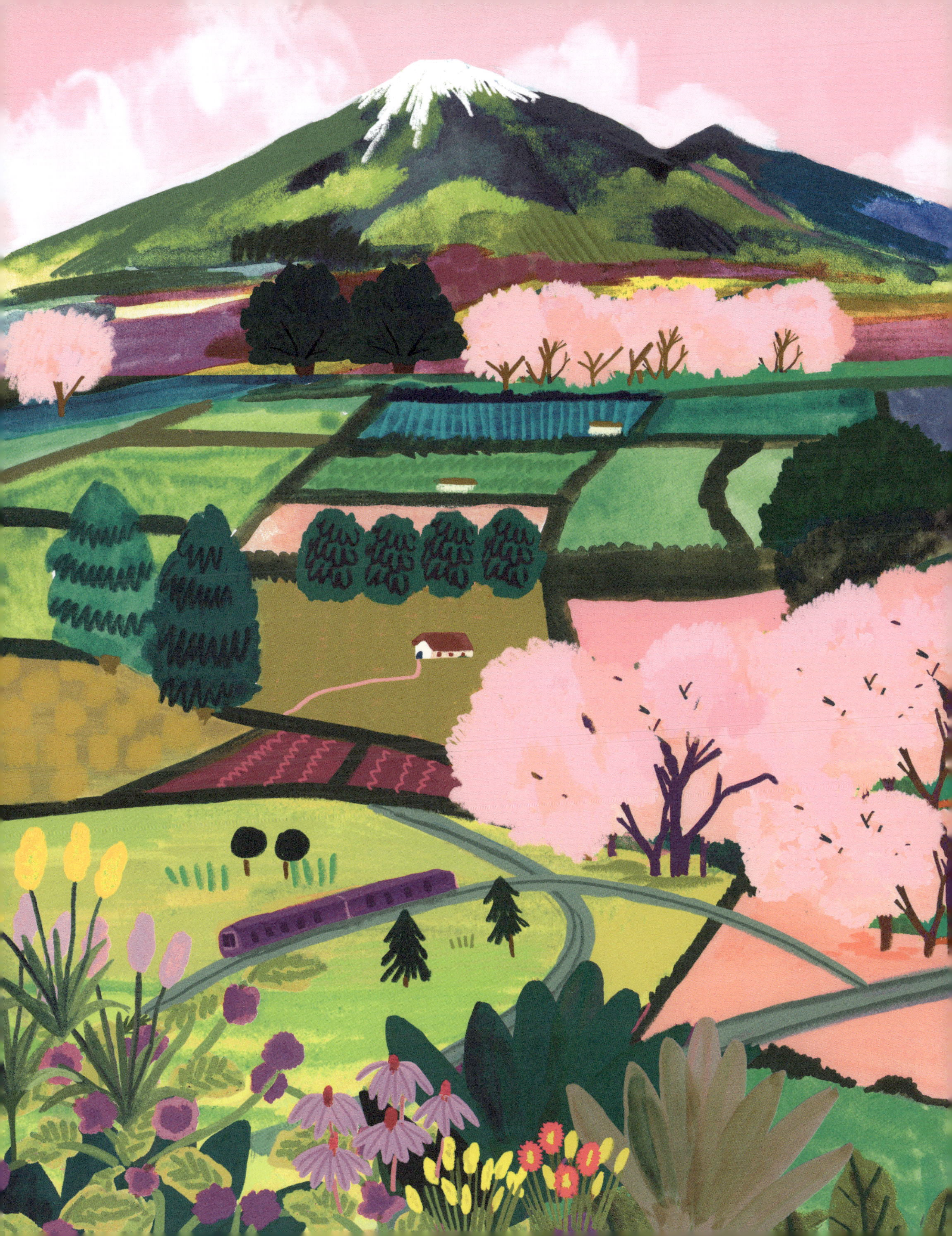

Train Ride in Japan

Picture yourself gazing out of the window of a train taking you through rural Japan. Fields of rice, swathes of lavender, cherry trees in full blossom, lush green terraces and patches of wildflowers, and of course, majestic Mount Fuji. Nature's patchwork of colors is a delight to paint, and the varying textures and shapes add another dimension of interest.

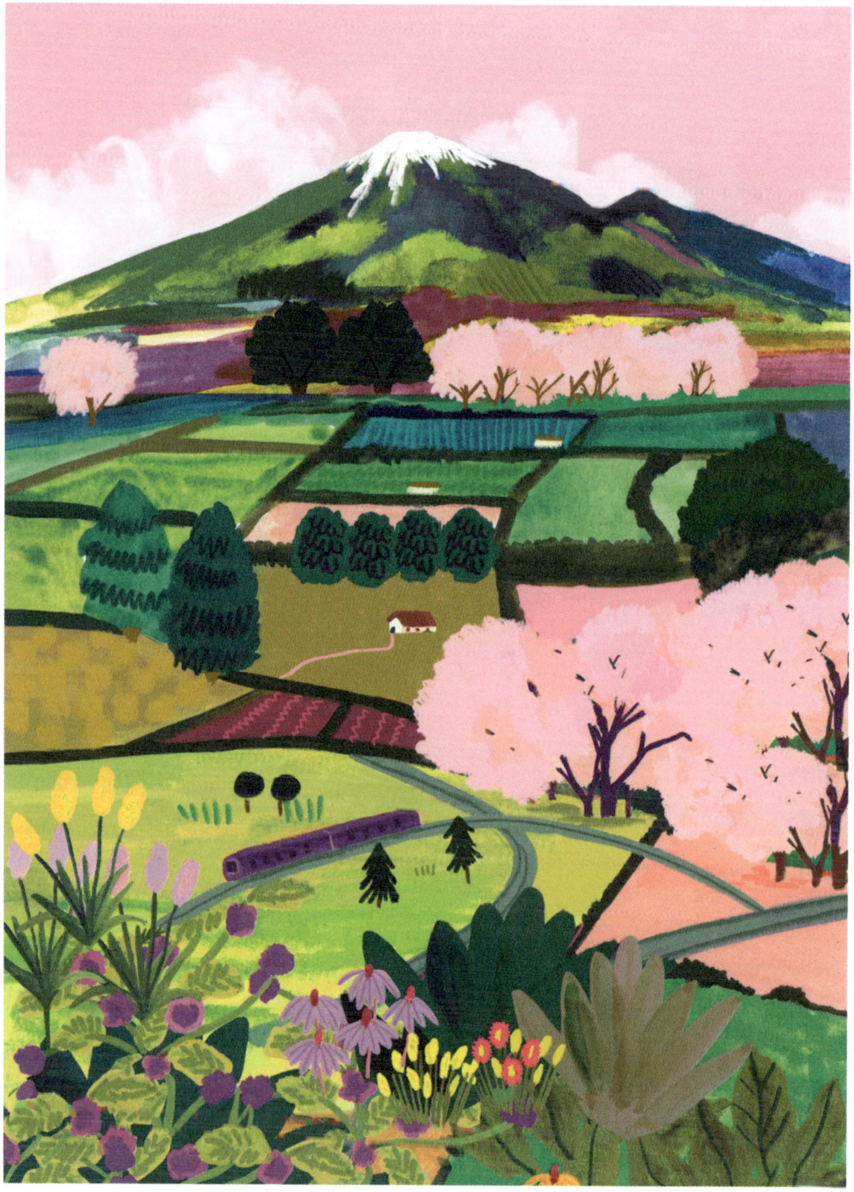

STEP BY STEP

- Start with the pink sky and cherry blossom
- Apply different greens to the fields and mountain
- Fill in the purples of the fields, train and flowers
- Finish with the remaining flower and tree details

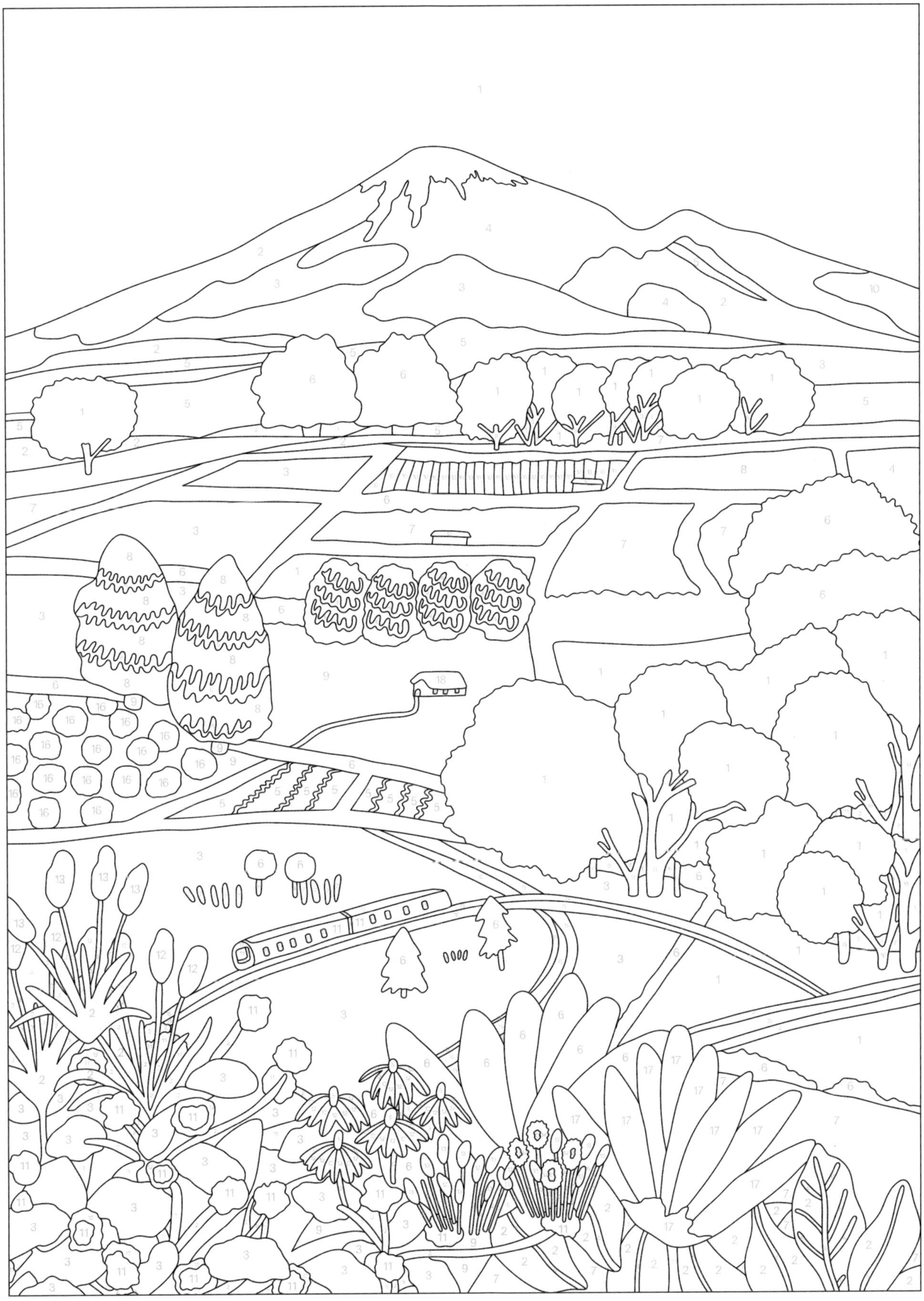

RAINBOW MOUNTAIN, PERU

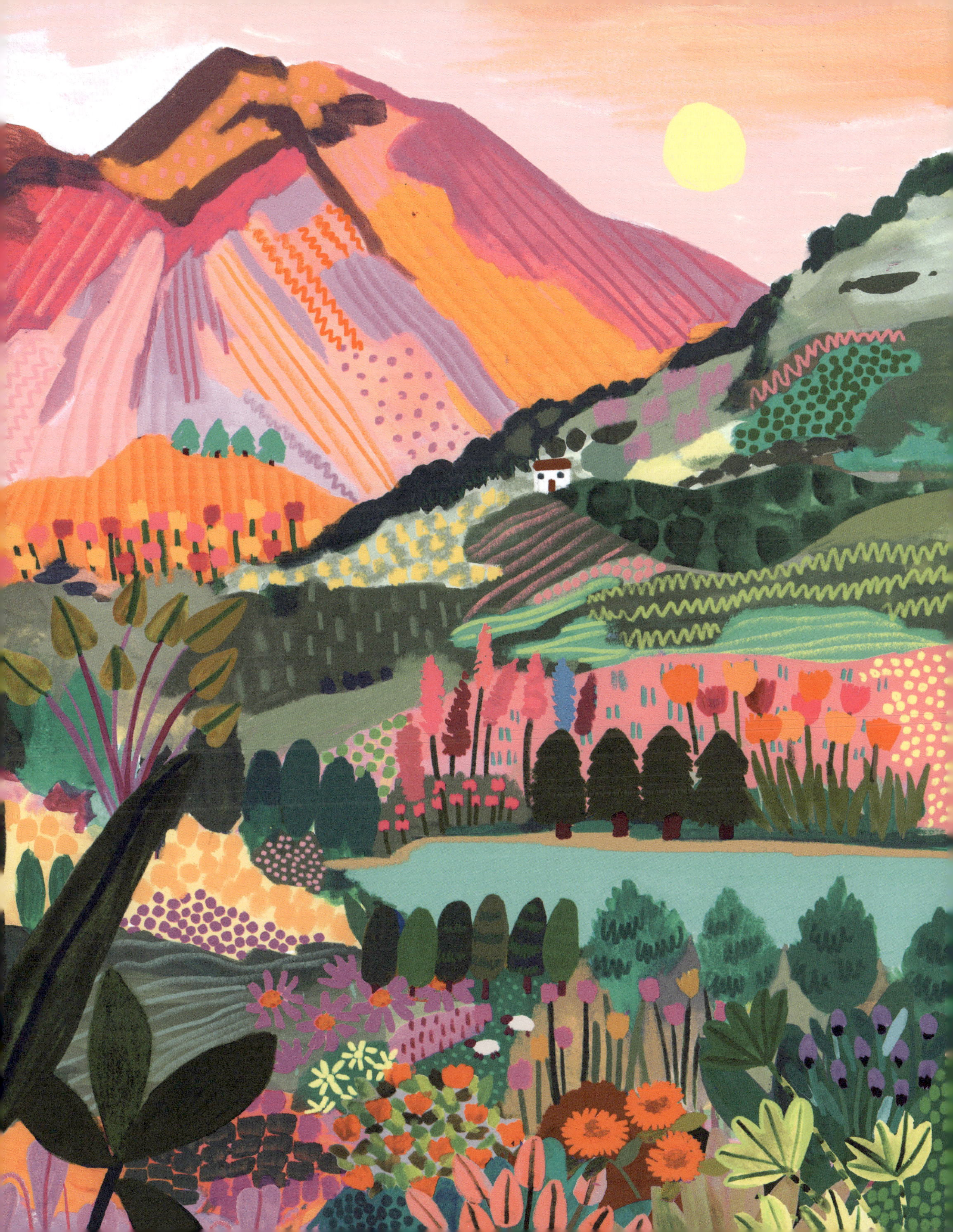

Rainbow Mountain, Peru

The Rainbow Mountain in Peru is truly a wonder. Formed over millions of years, it looks like a distinctly striped tapestry thanks to countless layers of mineral deposits. It is utterly other-worldly and has to be seen to be believed. Until then, flex your color palette and enjoy the wealth of hues and textures in front of you.

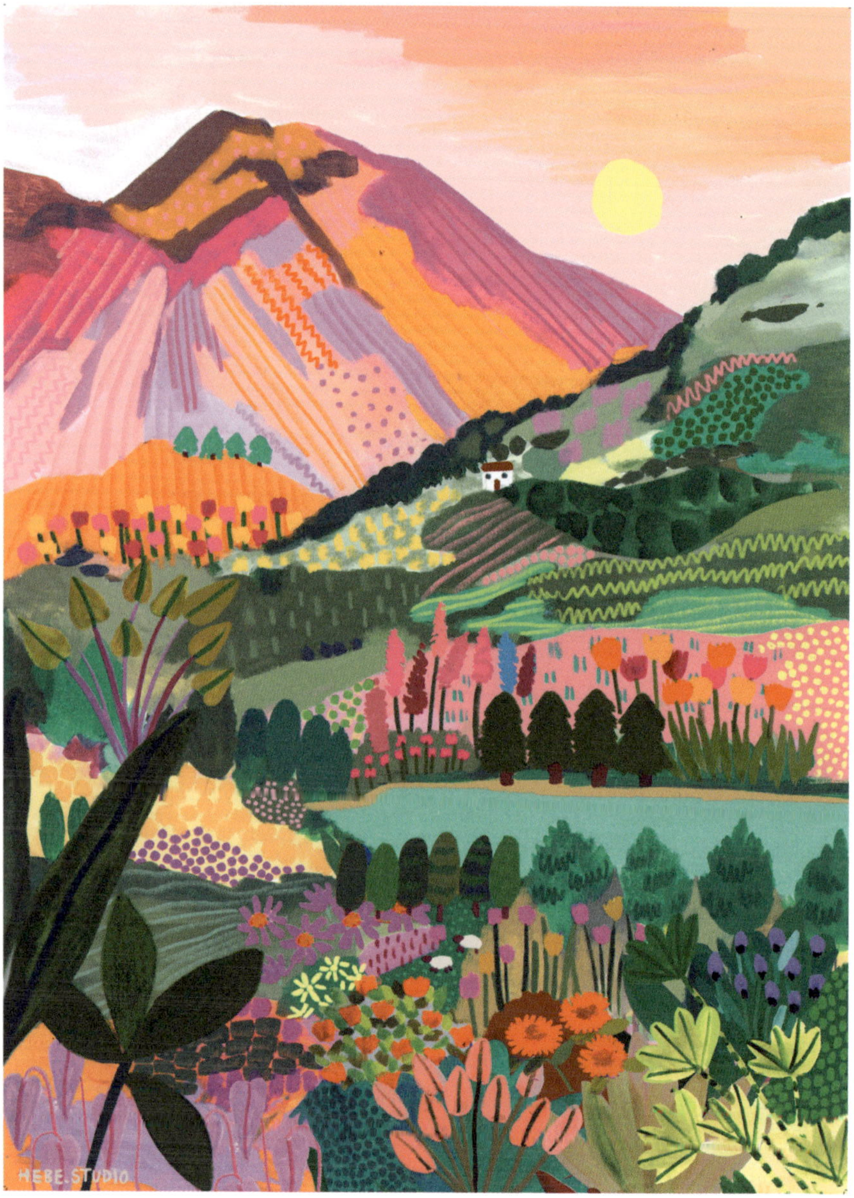

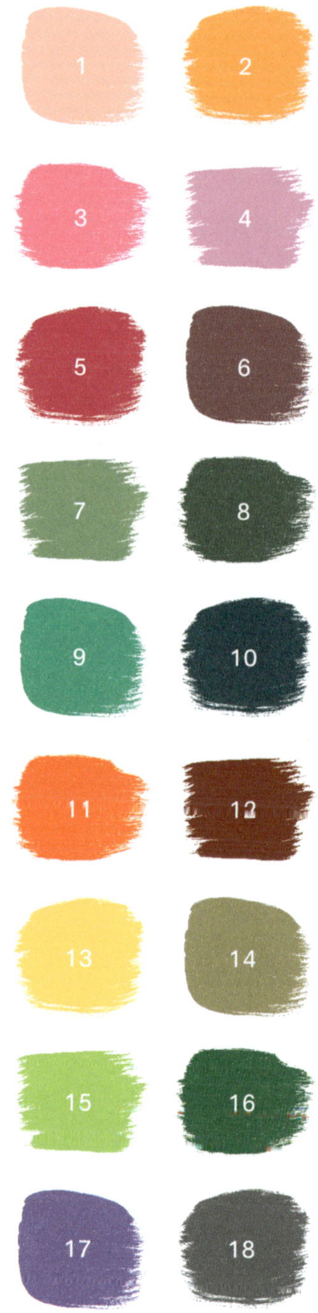

STEP BY STEP

- Fill in the pinks of the sky
- Move on to the pinks and oranges of the mountain
- Add in the variety of greens over the terrain
- Finish with the vegetation, flowers and sun

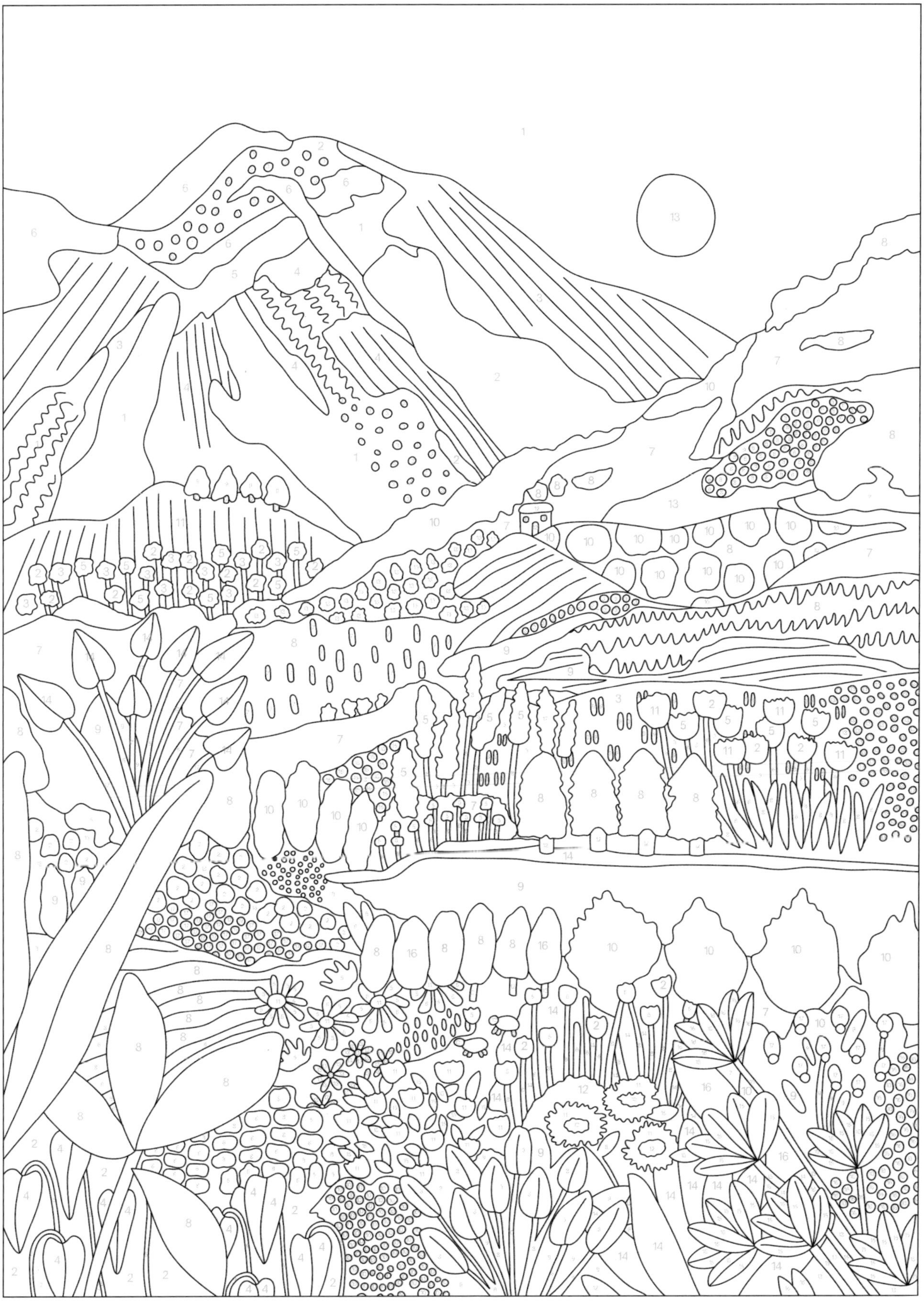

LEMONS IN ATRANI, ITALY

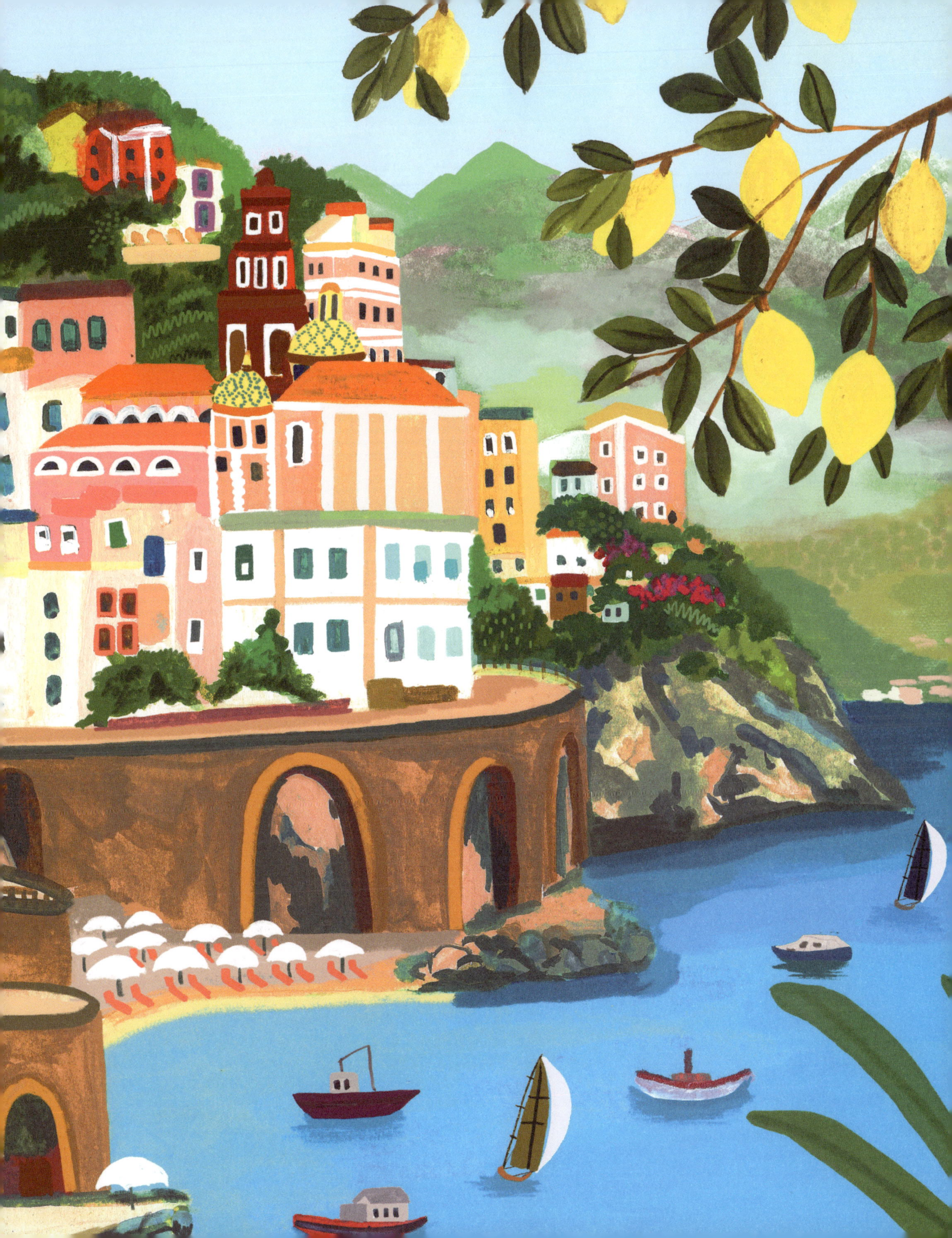

Lemons in Atrani, Italy

Considered the smallest town in Italy, Atrani boasts a prime spot on the Amalfi coast. Presided over by the Santa Maria Maddalene church with its distinctive bell tower, it is just as well loved for its production of the lemons that enjoy protected status on this stretch of coast. The lemons are as delicious as you'd expect and are enjoyed in the local cuisine and, of course, in limoncello.

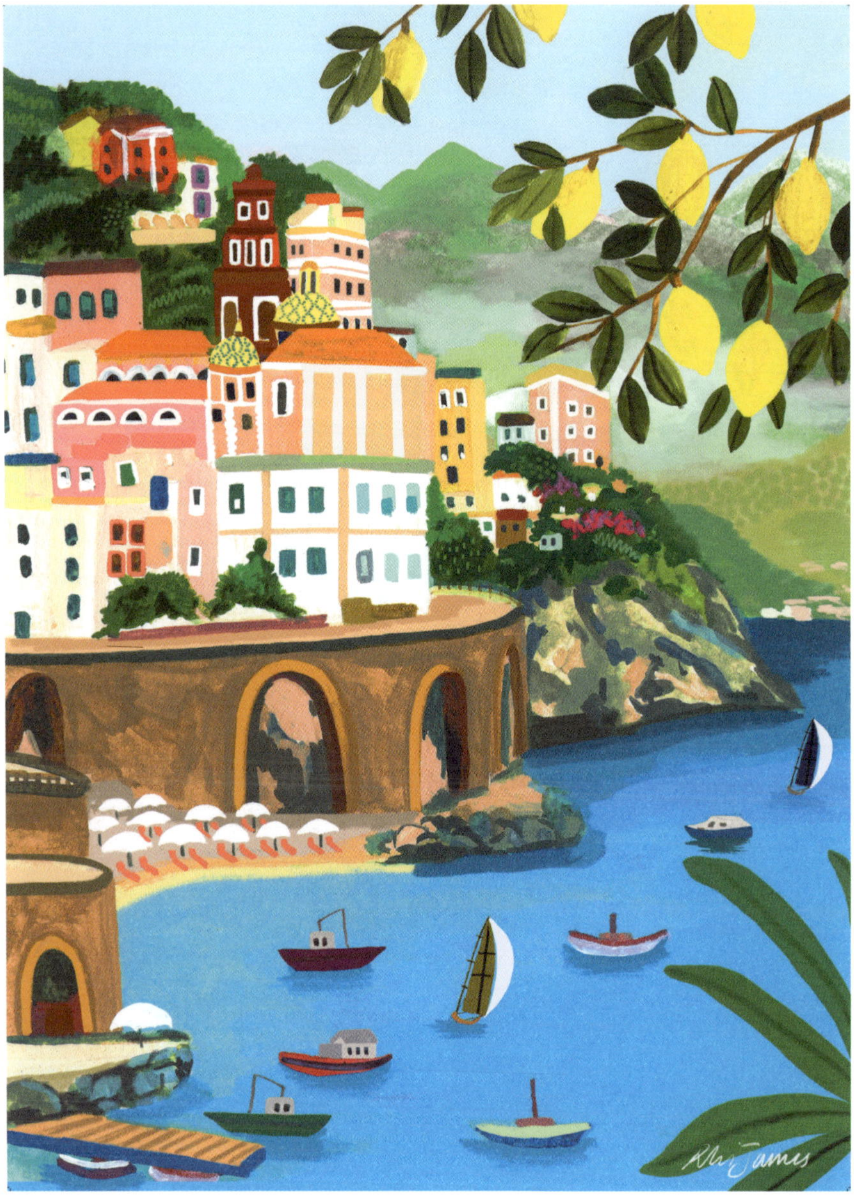

STEP BY STEP

- Start with the blue sea and the dappled shades in the distance
- Next, fill in the bridge with its arches
- Now do the buildings and their windows
- Finish with the boats, greenery and lemons

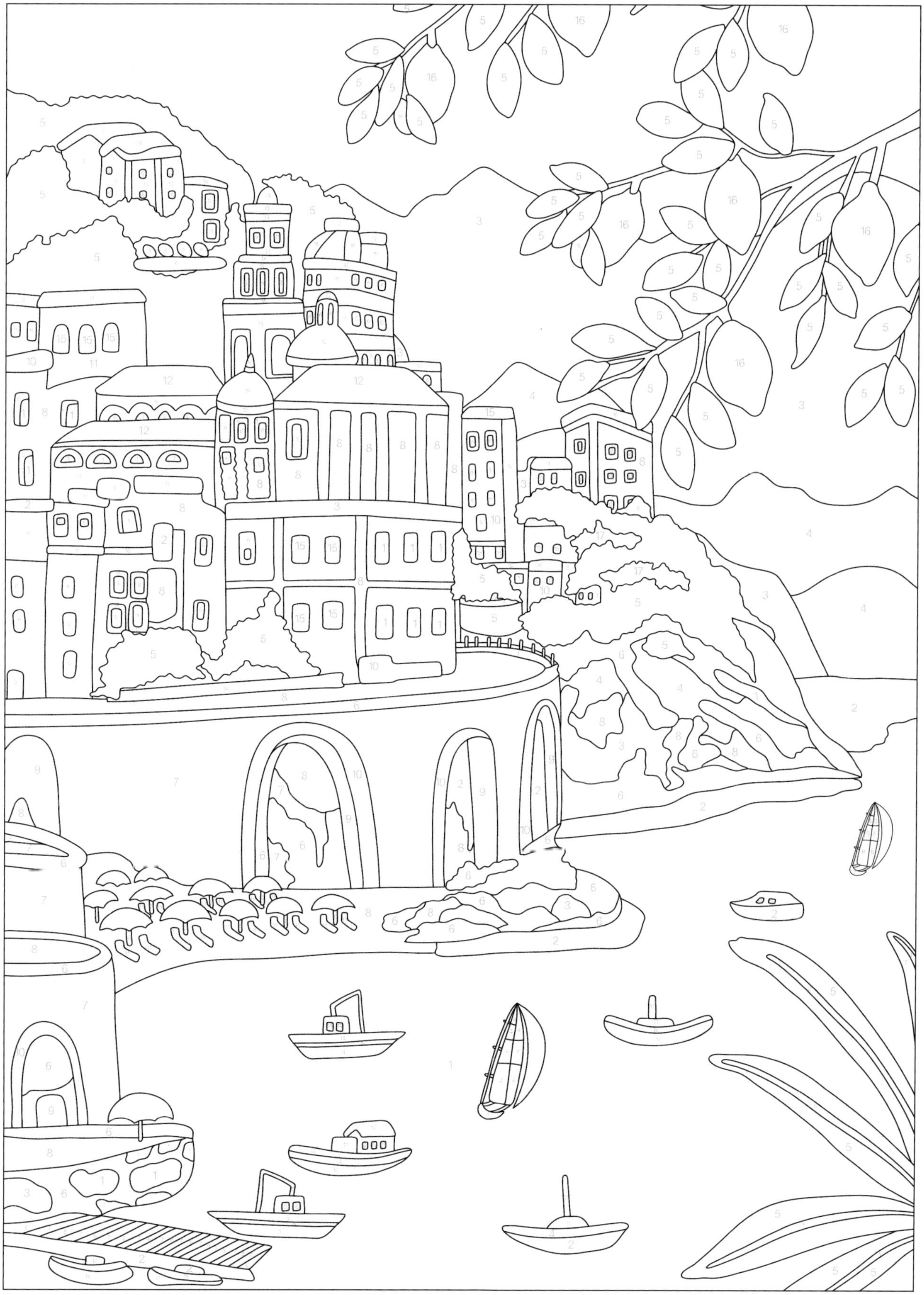

MOUNT COOK, NEW ZEALAND

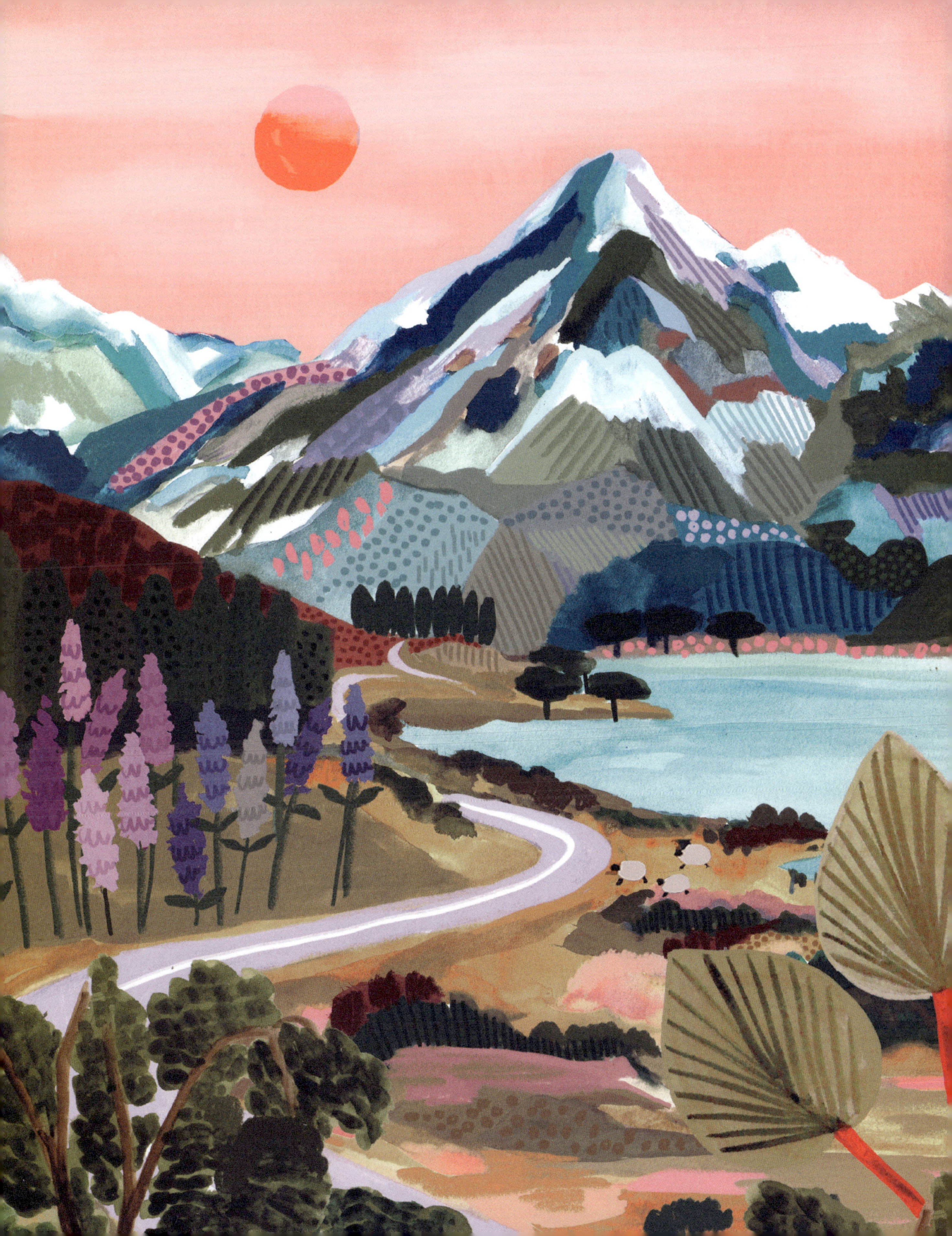

Mount Cook, New Zealand

Giving its name to both a UNESCO World Heritage national park and the mountain within it that is New Zealand's highest, Mount Cook is a unique landscape of rock and ice. It's home to lupins, wilding pines, the unusually named vegetable sheep plant that coats the rocks, and the Mount Cook buttercup – the largest buttercup in the world! There are plenty of visually interesting glacial details to capture in this breathtaking scene.

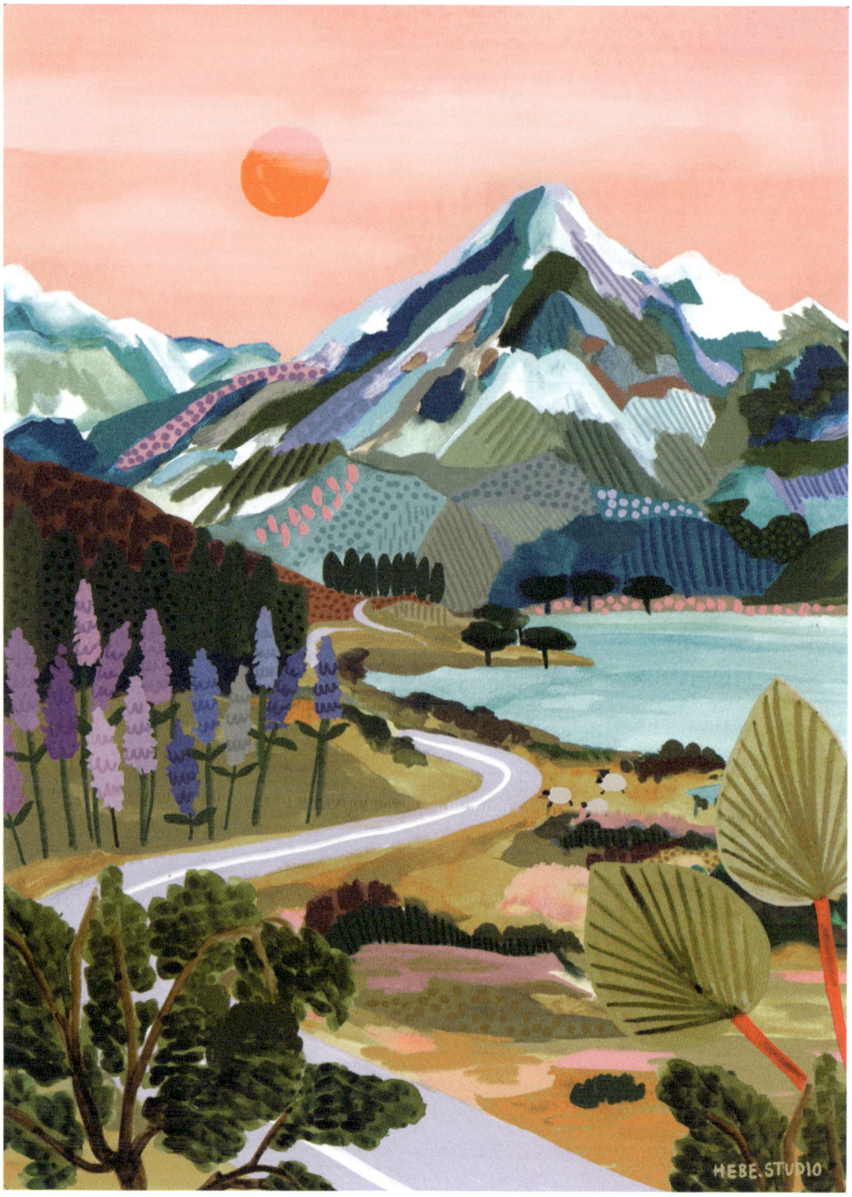

STEP BY STEP

- Start with the pink of the sky
- Fill in the icy blues of the mountain and lake
- Add the browns and greens dotted around the scene
- Finish with the leaves, flowers, road and sun

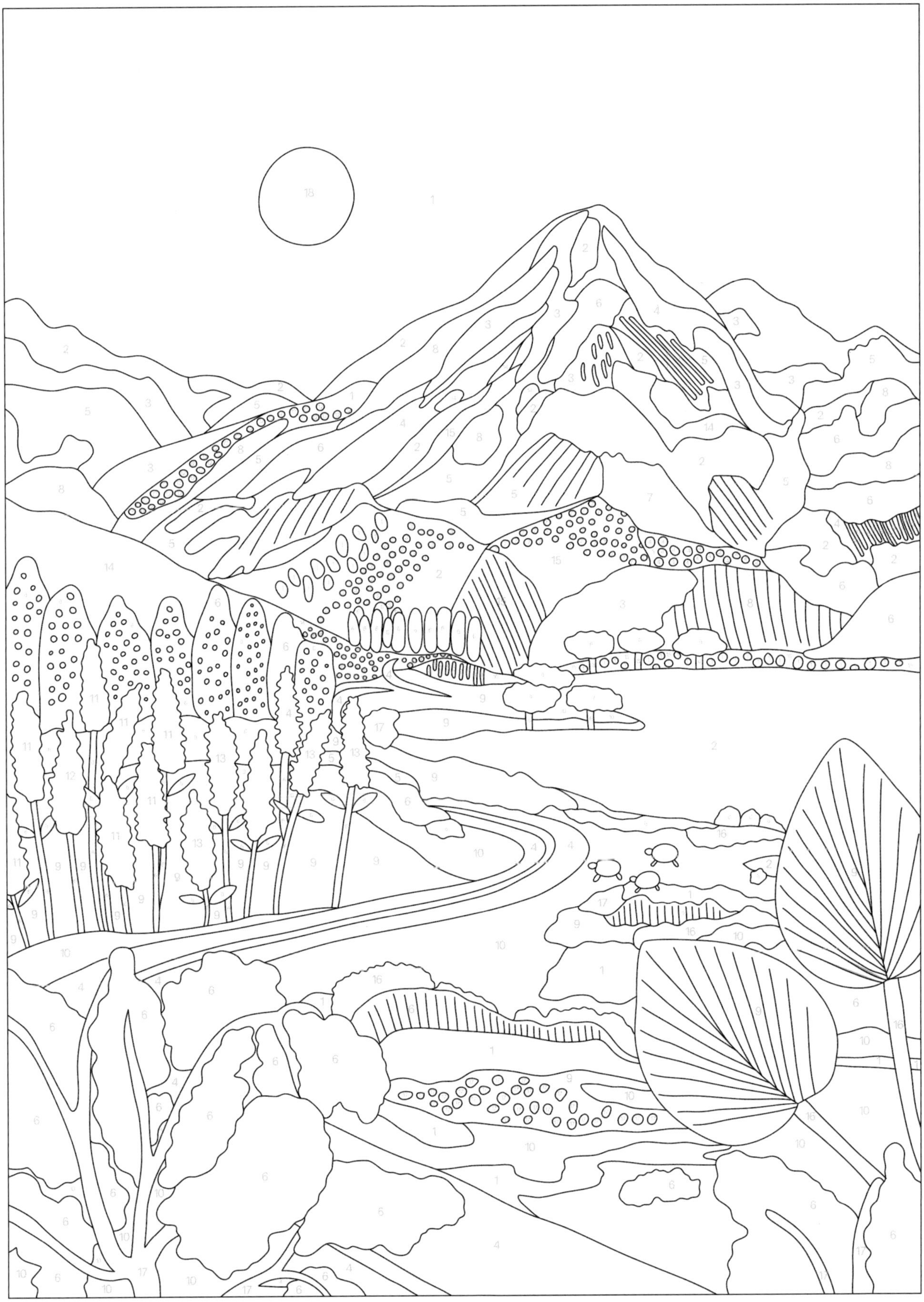

BEACH BUTTERFLY, SRI LANKA

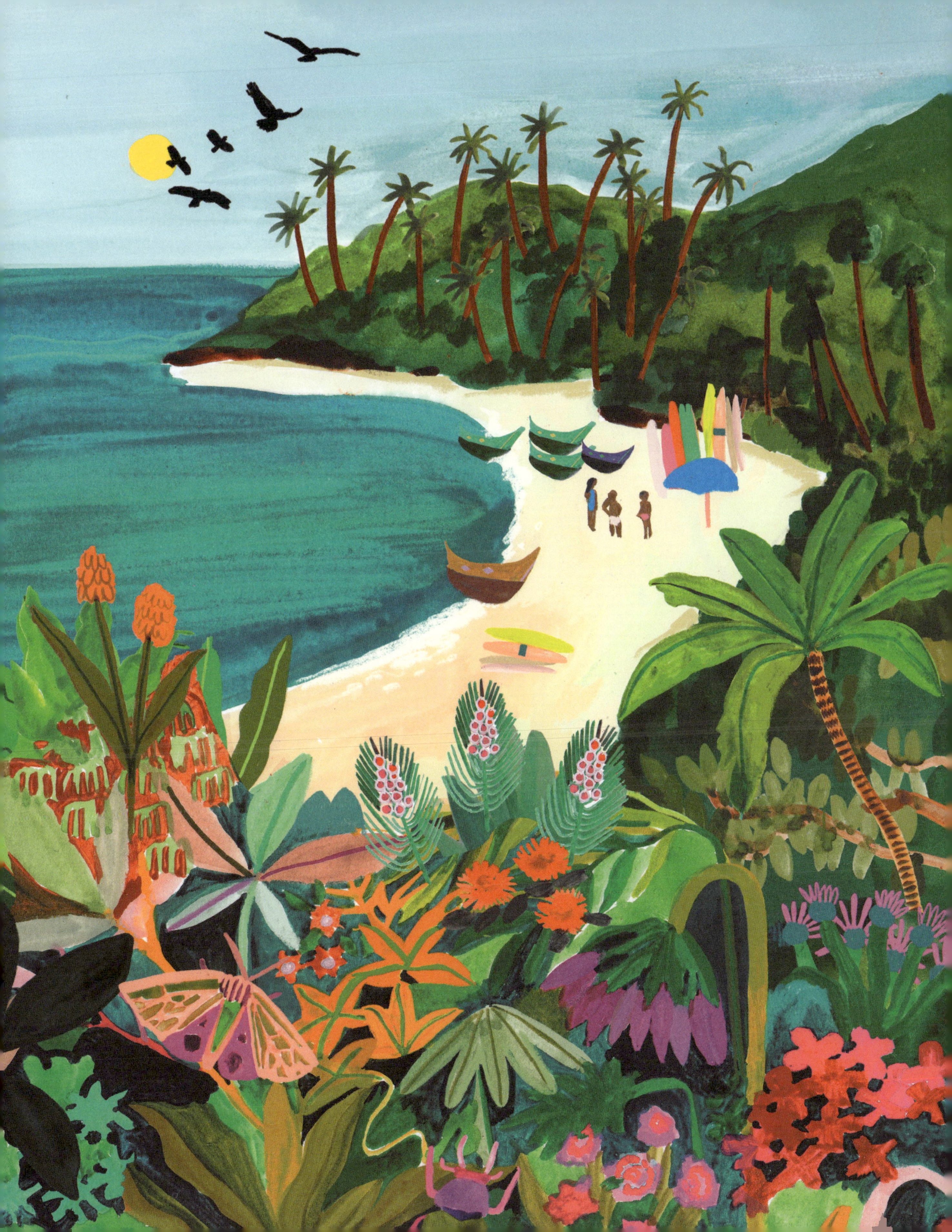

Beach Butterfly, Sri Lanka

Whether you come to an idyllic horseshoe bay like this for the surfing, the sun worshipping, to watch the fishermen or just to let all your troubles melt away, you'll find a treasure trove of natural beauty to explore. From sea turtles and monkeys to butterflies and multi-colored vegetation all around, you'll never run out of sights, sounds and smells to enjoy.

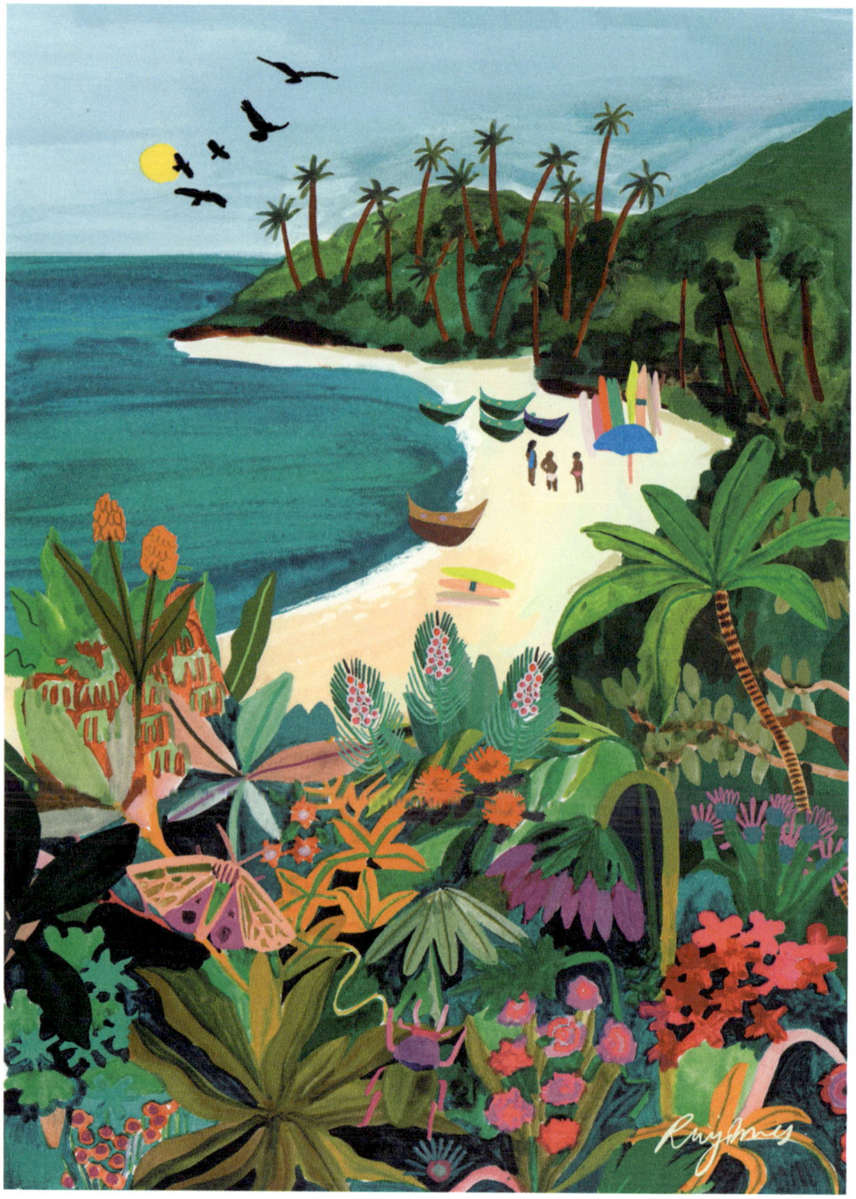

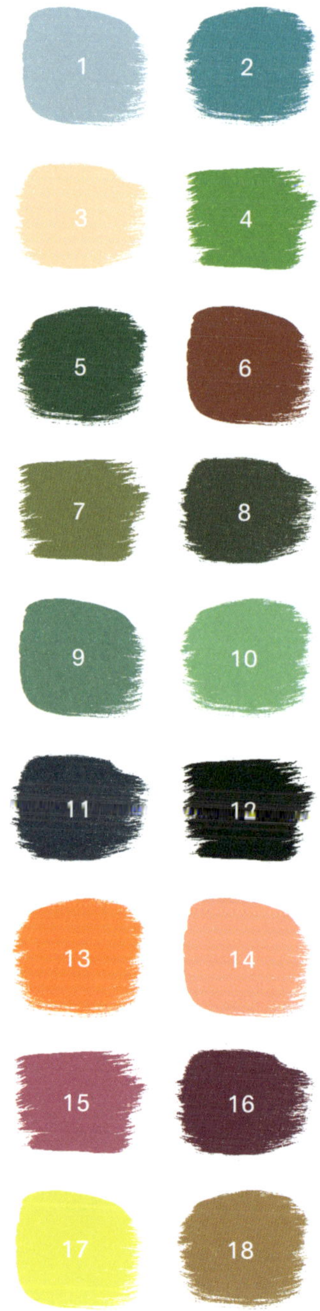

STEP BY STEP

- Start with the blues of the sky and sea
- Do the sandy beach next
- Fill in the greens of the cliffs and vegetation
- Finish with the flowers, beach details, birds and sun

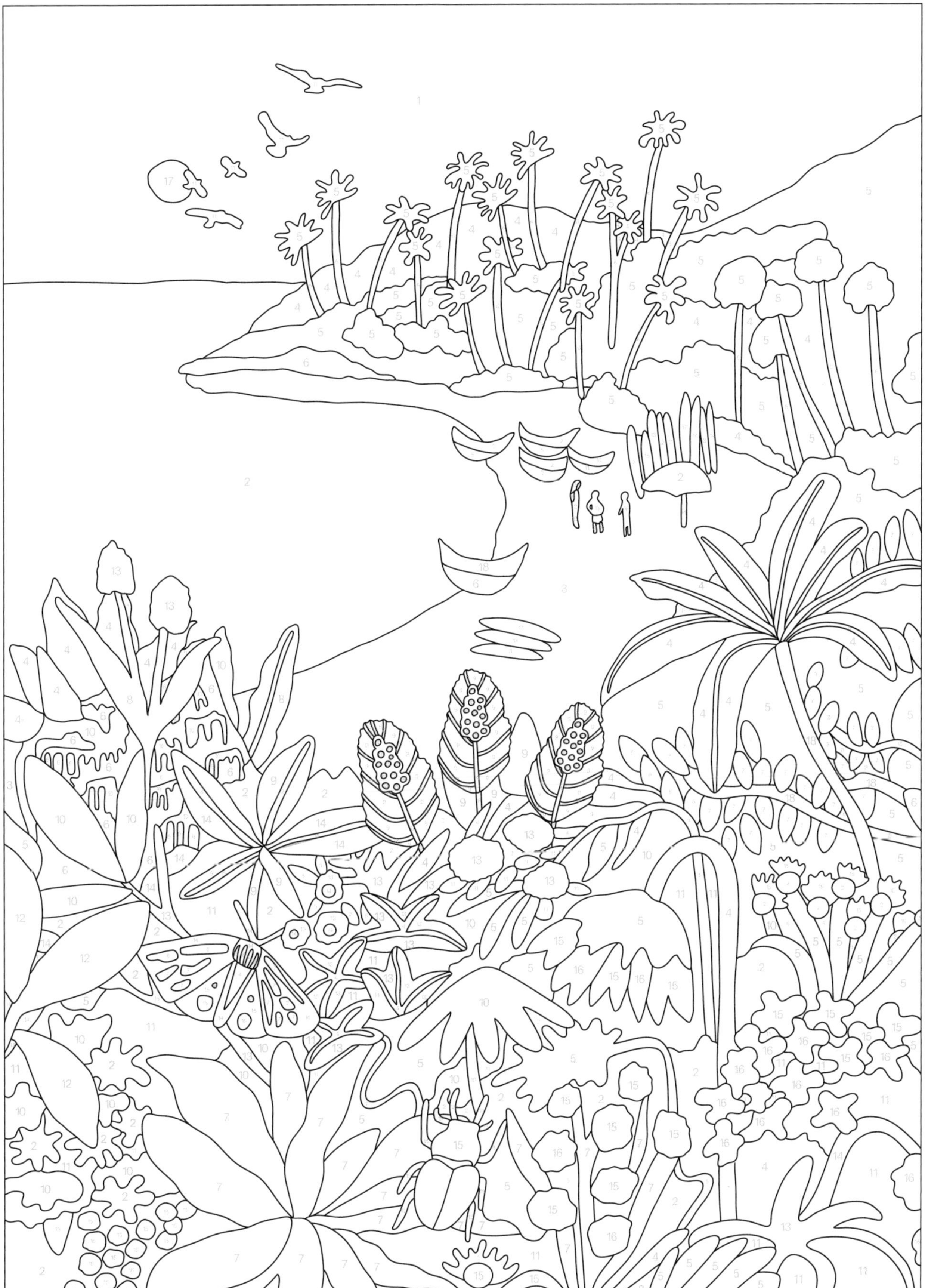

CACTUS MOUNTAINS, USA

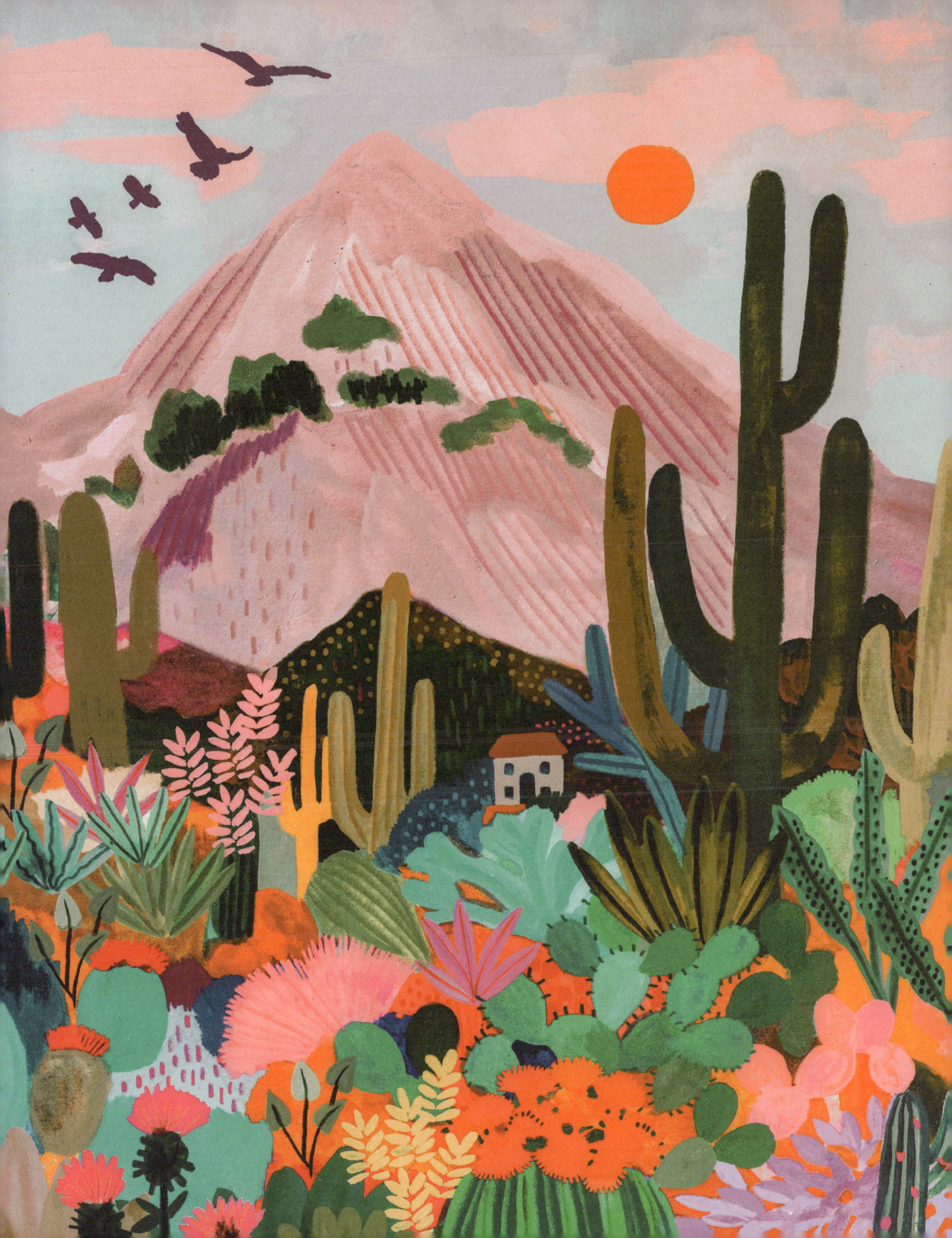

Cactus Mountains, USA

Perhaps surprisingly, the climate in Arizona's Sonoran desert – a combination of heat and rainfall patterns – allows many plants to thrive there. One of the most memorable features of this desert is the proliferation of saguaro – large, tree-like cacti that can take decades to grow to any size. Combine these eerie creatures with the mountainous landscape and you have a fascinating tableau to recreate at home.

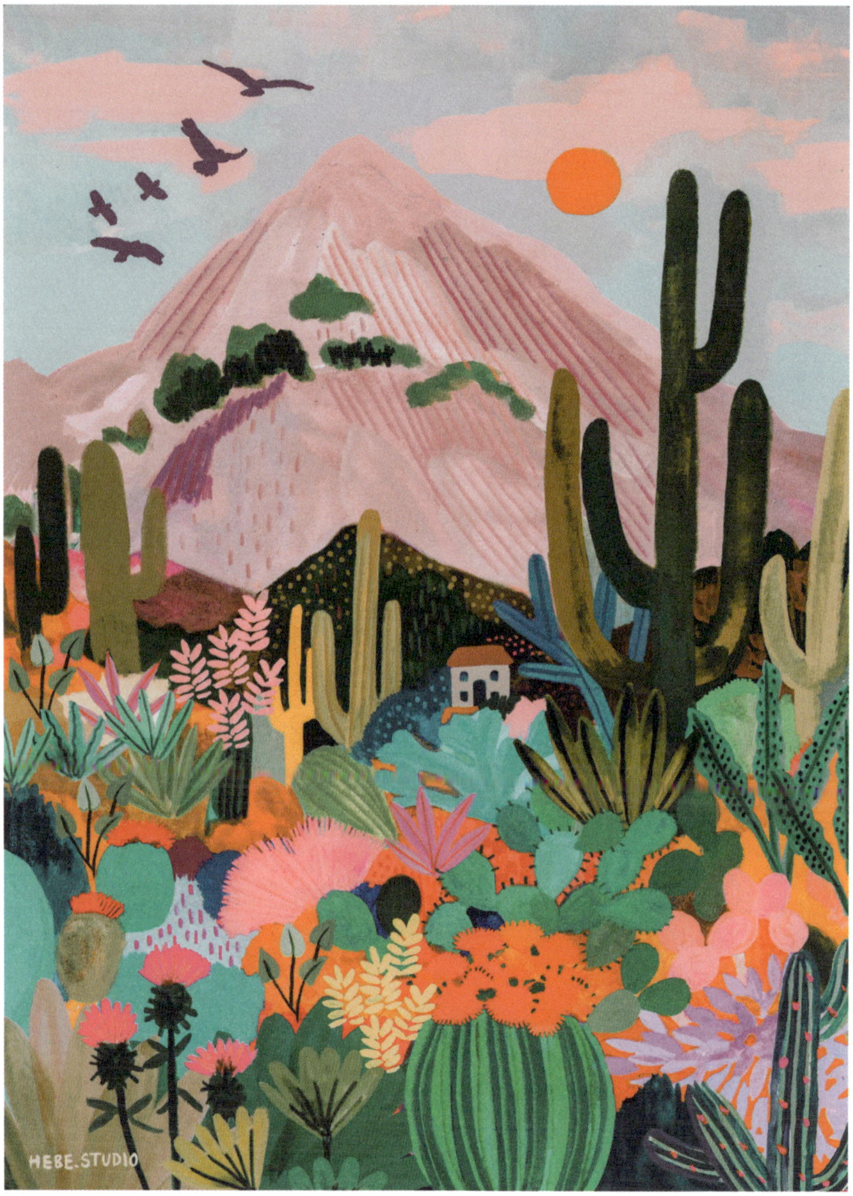

STEP BY STEP

- Start with the pink and blue of the sky
- Next, focus on the pink mountain
- Move on to the greens of the cacti and other leaves
- Fill in the flowers, birds and sun

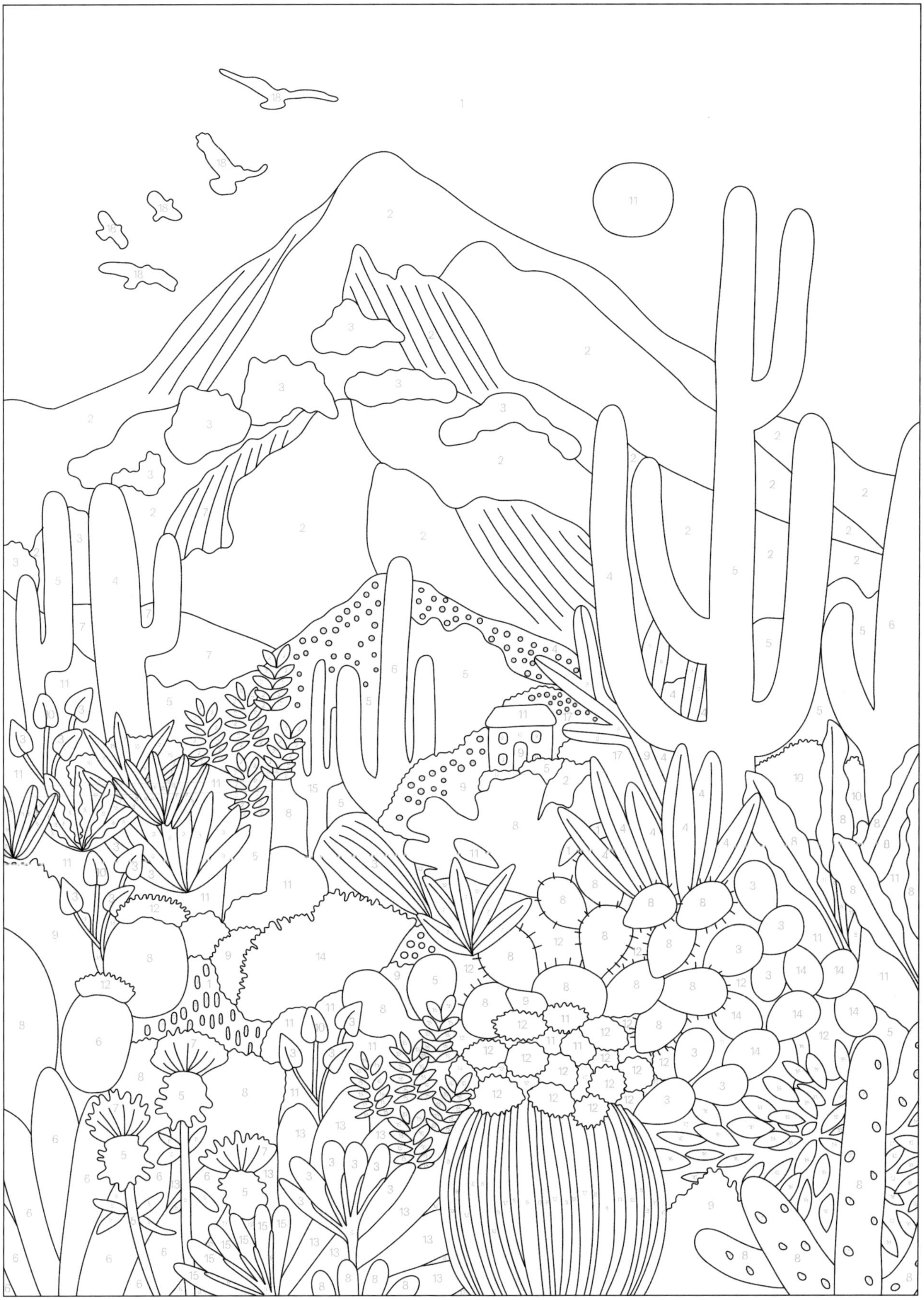

CINQUE TERRE, ITALY

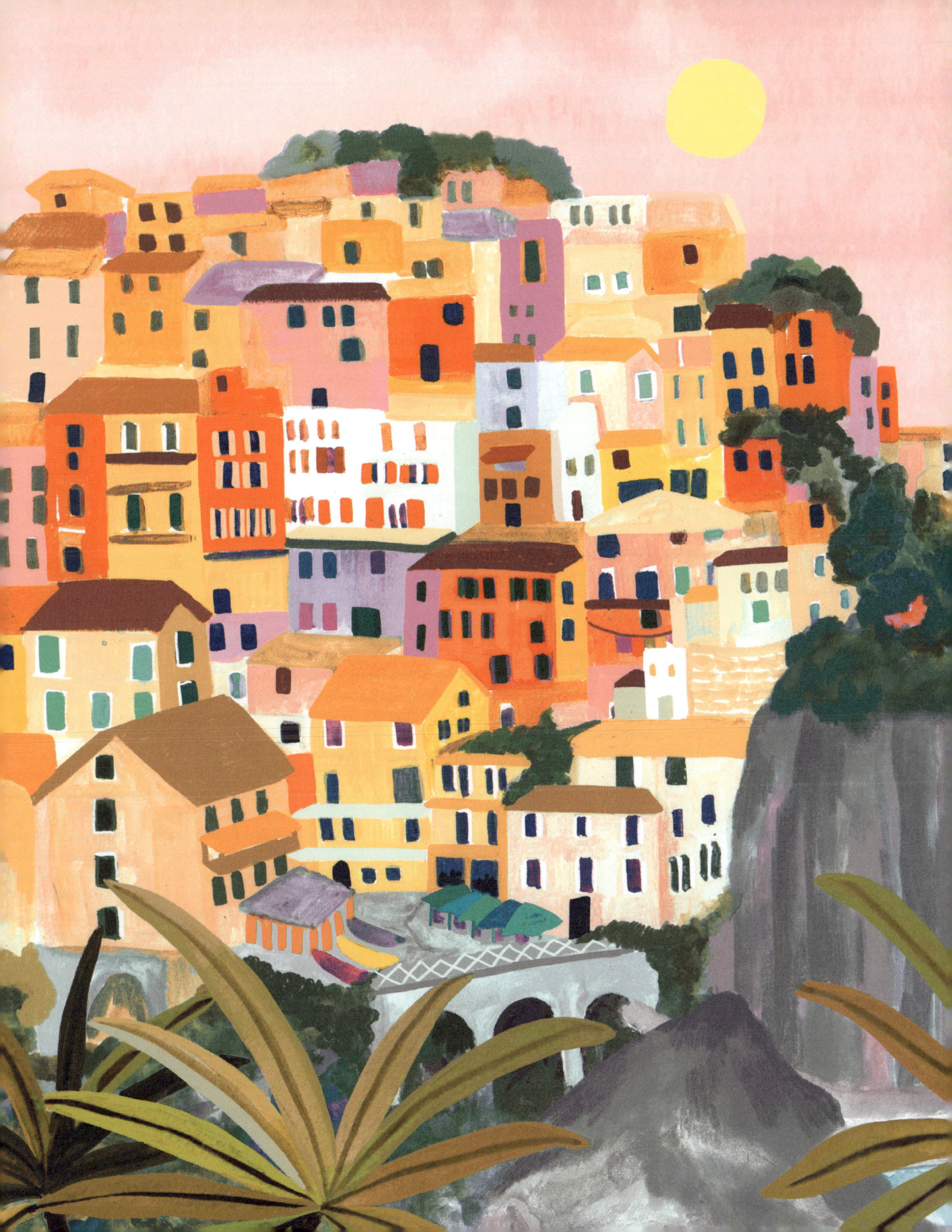

Cinque Terre, Italy

Cinque Terre, or 'Five Lands', is made up of five villages in Liguria on the north-western coast of Italy, characterized by their clifftop houses in a rainbow of colors. It is so pretty that it's hard to believe this is a real place and what's more, a national park with walking trails and vineyards, as well as gravity-defying homes, bars and restaurants. A dream location for lovers of La Dolce Vita.

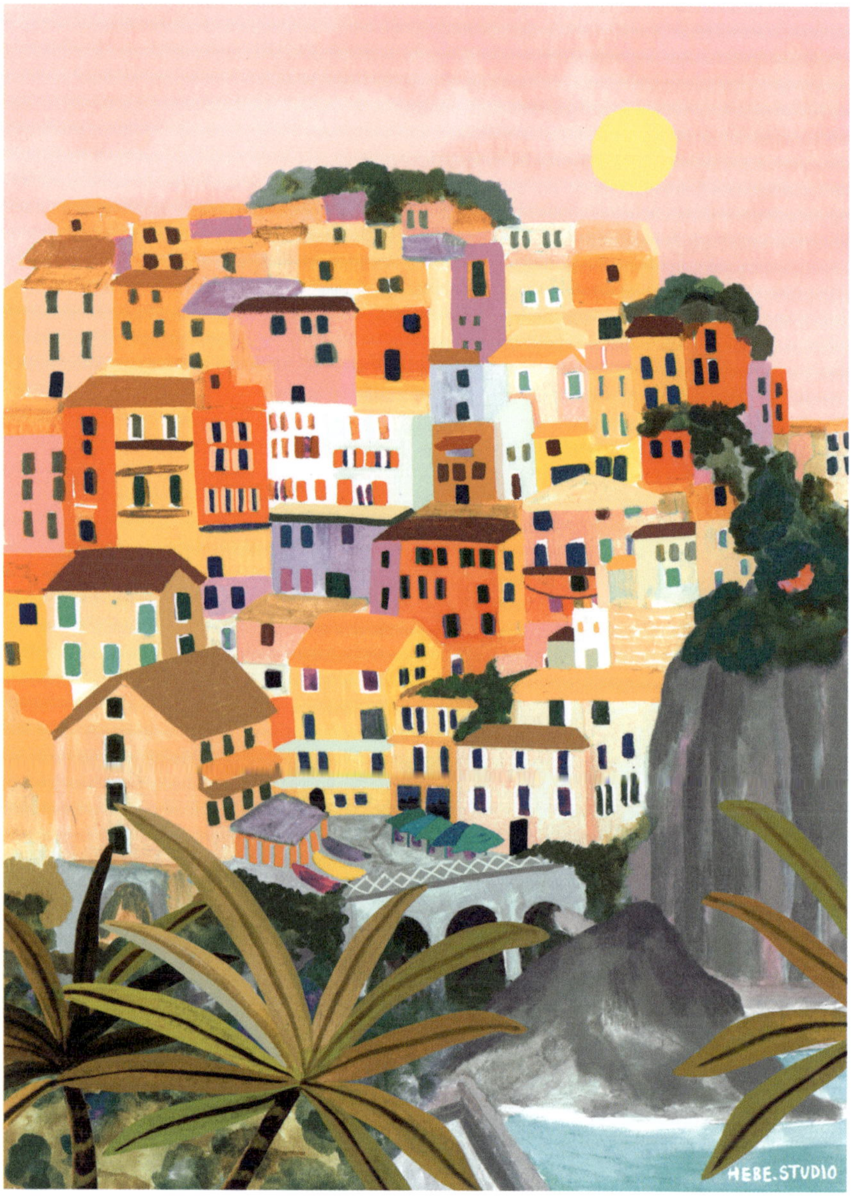

STEP BY STEP

- Start with the pink sky and grey rocks
- Move on to the blocks of color in the buildings
- Do the vegetation in the foreground
- Fill in the windows, sun and other details

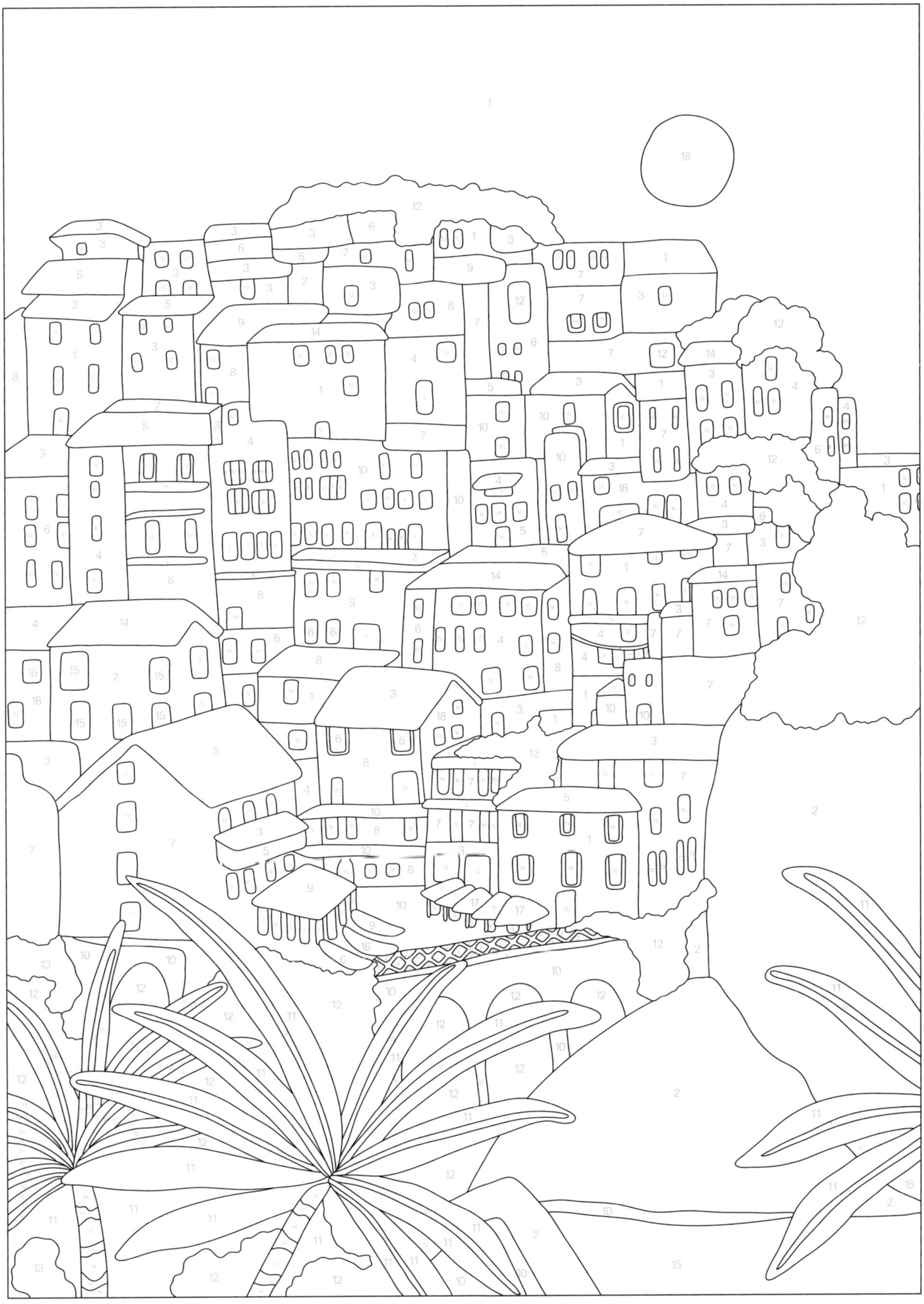

DOVE LAKE, AUSTRALIA

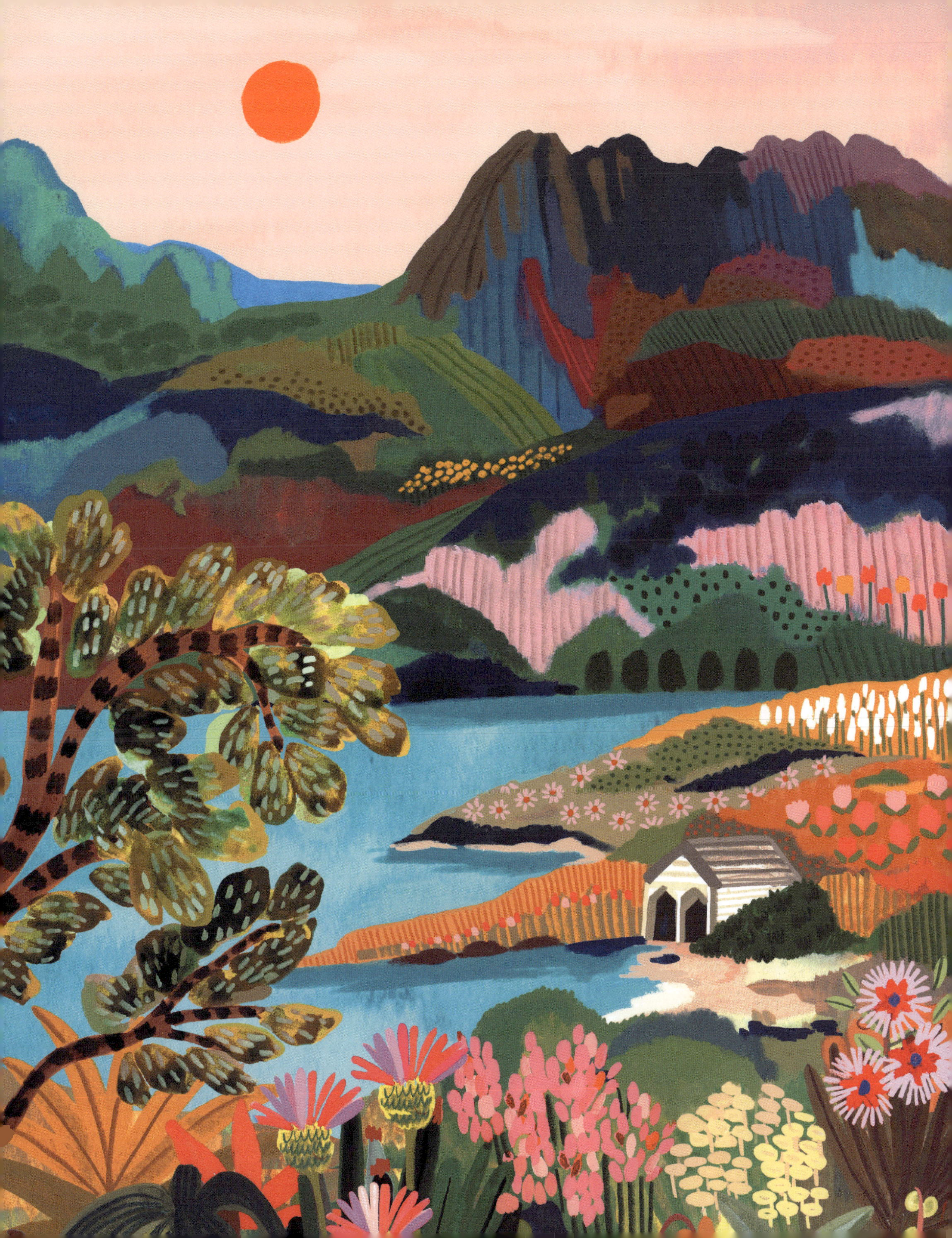

Dove Lake, Australia

Cradle Mountain in Tasmania is home to an extraordinary diversity of endemic flora. It makes for the most rewarding painting, thanks to the range of flowers, shrubs and trees, all encircling beautiful Dove Lake and the boat house that quietly stands guard on the water's edge. As you color in nature's shapes, know that you might encounter tanglefoot with its distinctive ridged leaves and Tasmanian waratah with its head of red, wispy petals.

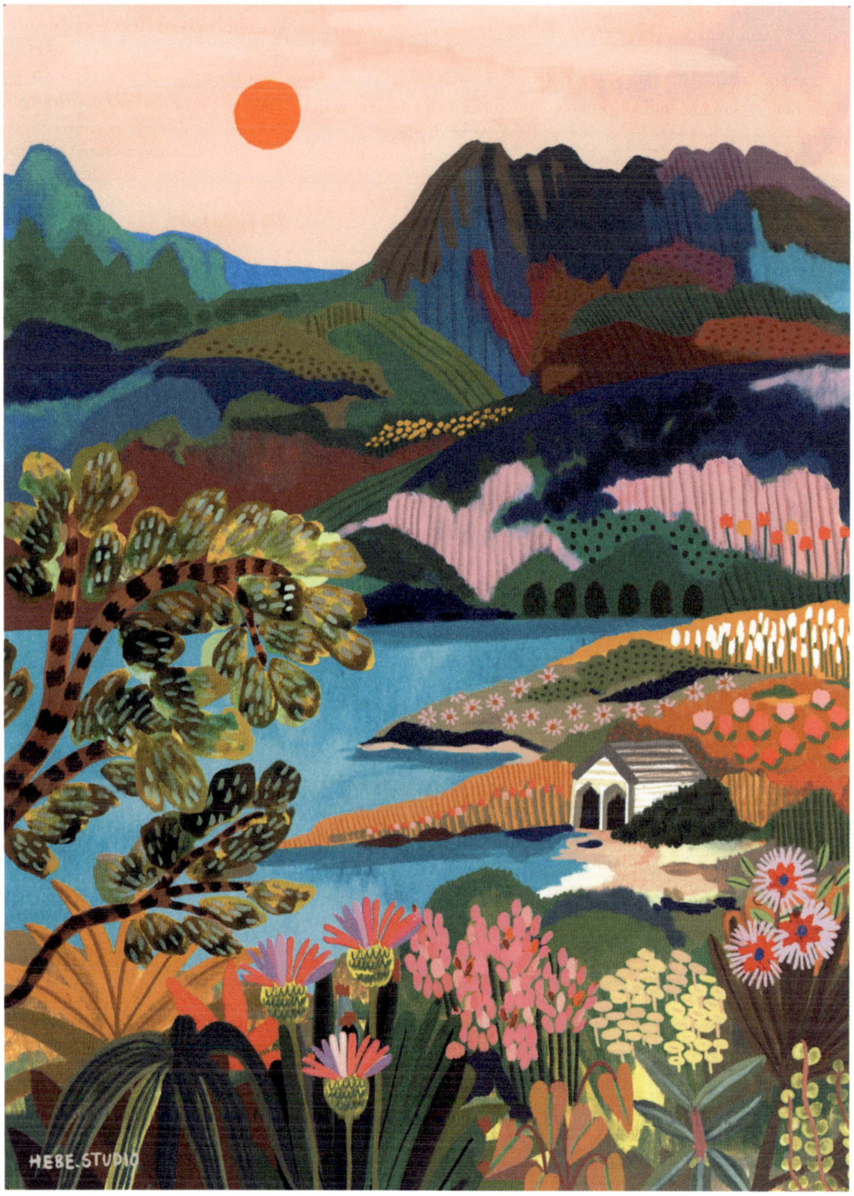

STEP BY STEP

- Start with the pink of the sky
- Fill in the blue of the water and parts of the mountain
- Add in the other colors of the mountain and terrain
- Finish with the vegetation, boat house and sun

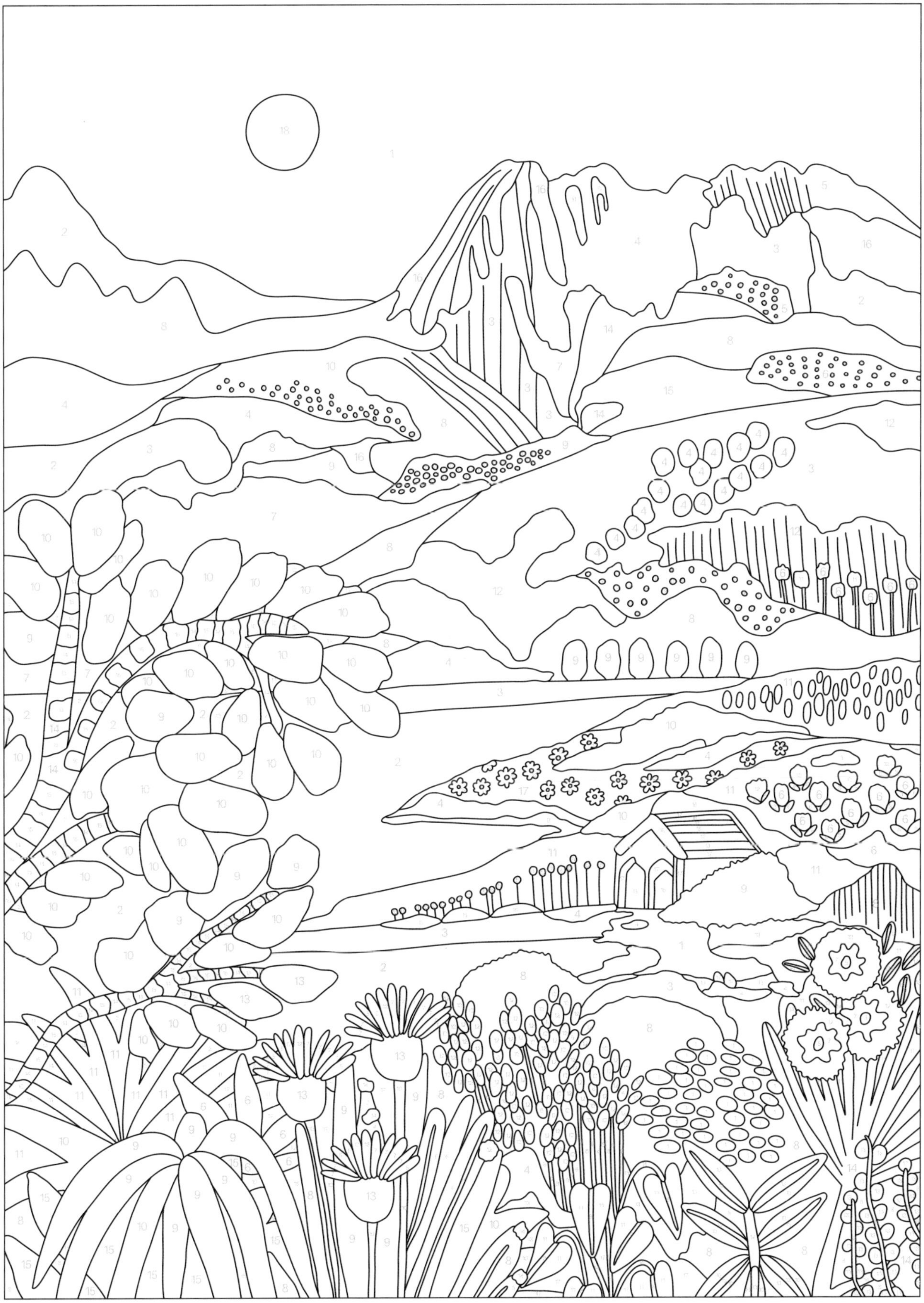

PUGLIA,
ITALY

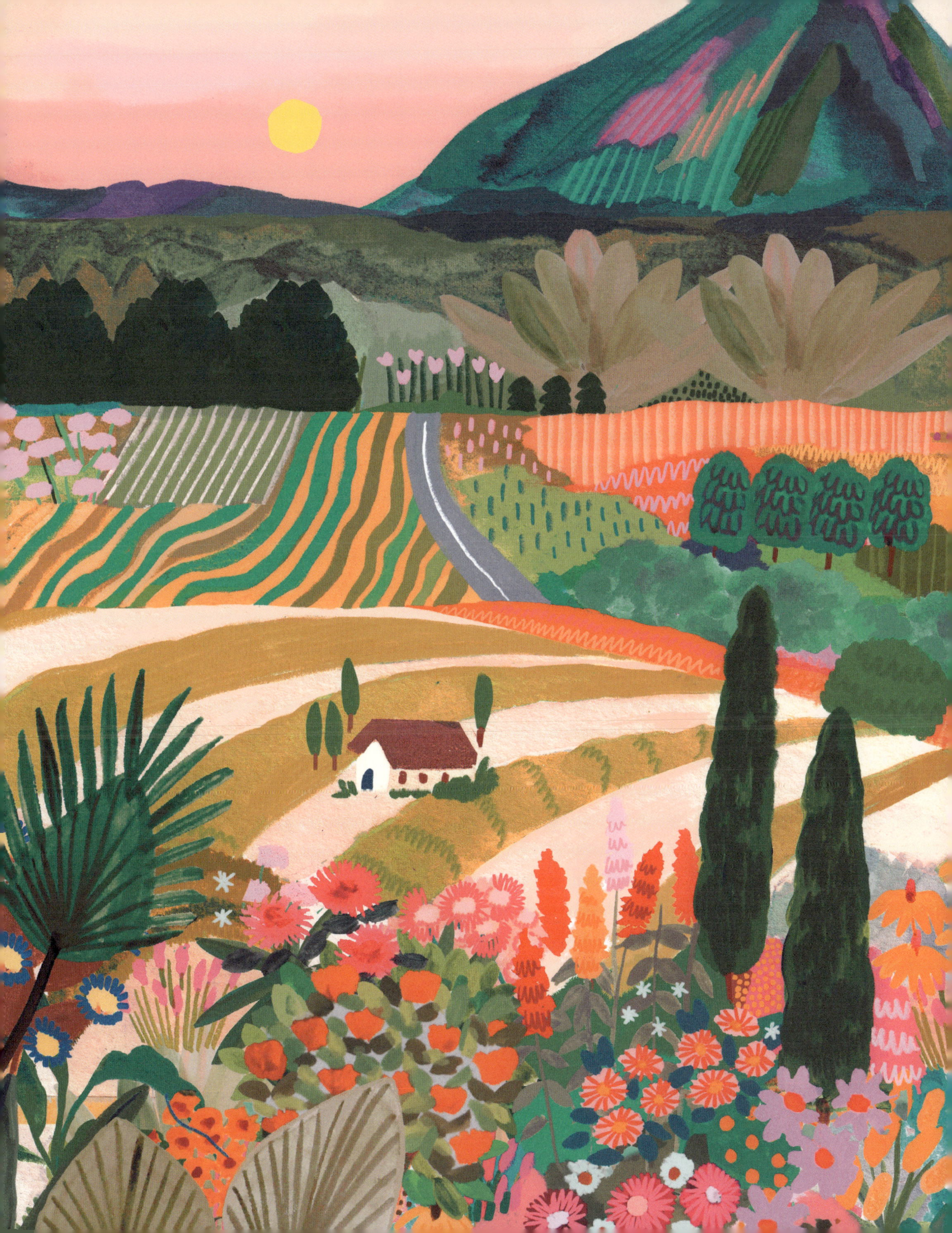

Puglia, Italy

Puglia, in the 'heel' of Italy, has some of the most spectacular countryside Italy has to offer. Farmhouses are dotted across the gently rolling hills, vineyards and olive groves abound, slim cypress trees cleave the natural curves of the land. You could easily lose yourself in the timeless romance of the place.

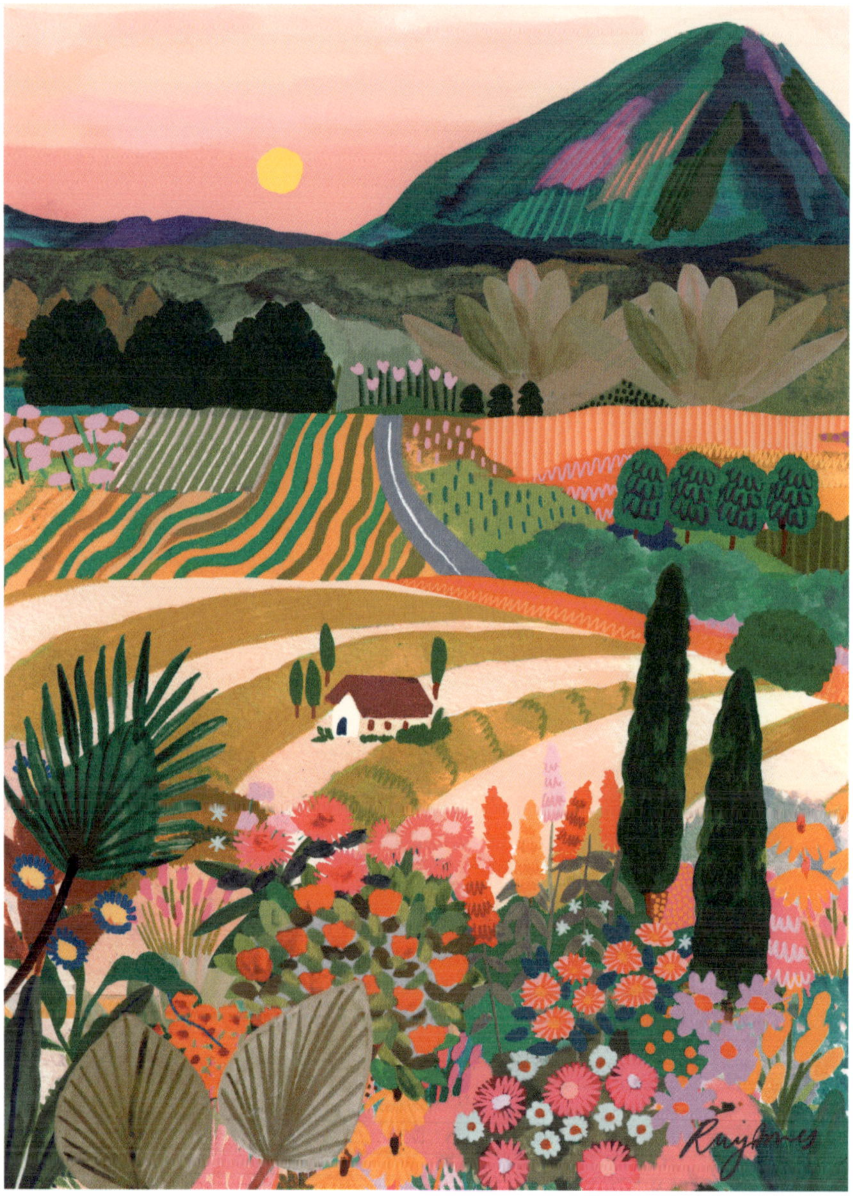

STEP BY STEP

- Start with the pink of sky
- Fill in the greens of the mountains in the background
- Move on to the striped fields in the centre and foreground
- Finish with the trees, flowers, farmhouse and sun

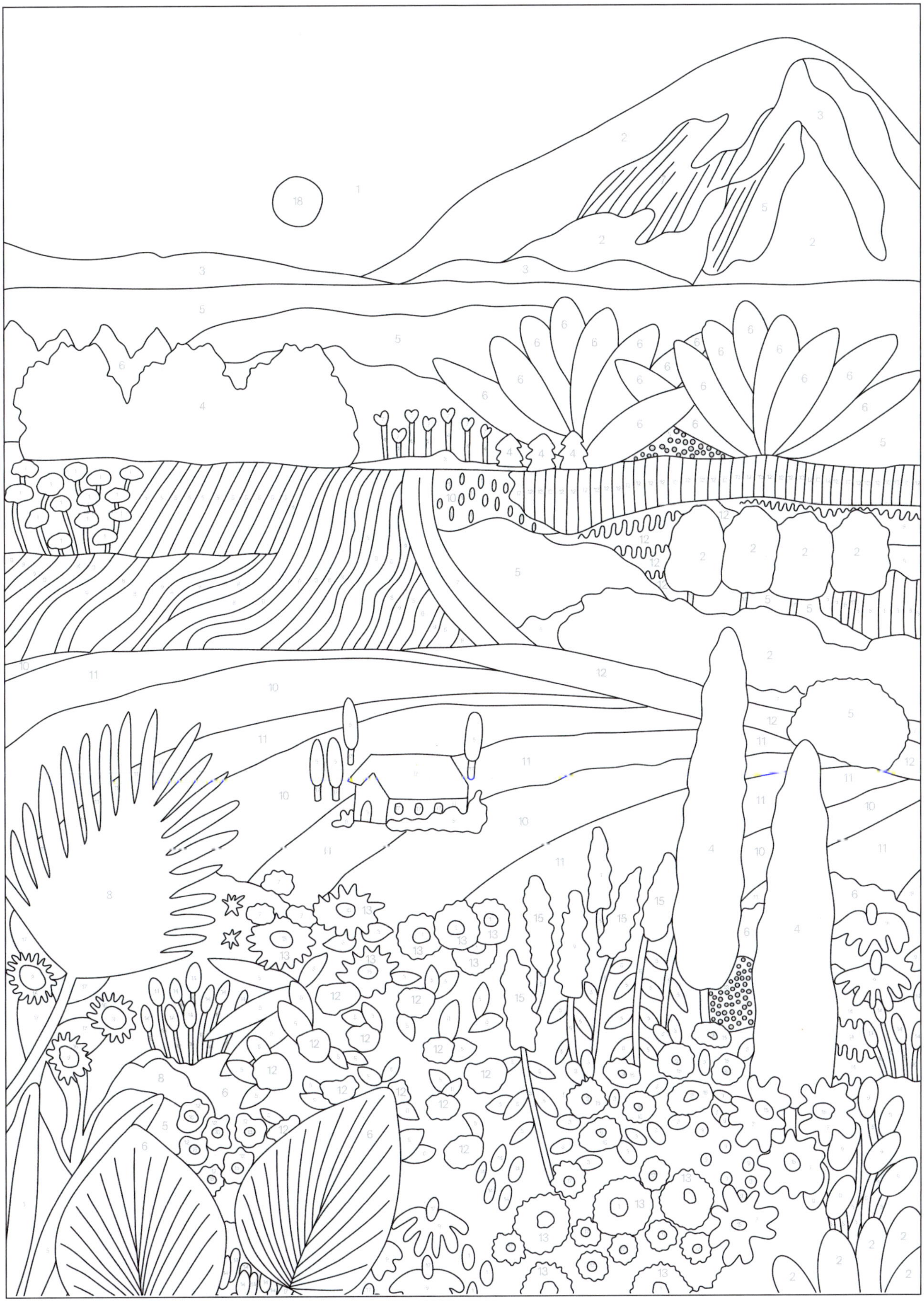

SNOWDON, WALES

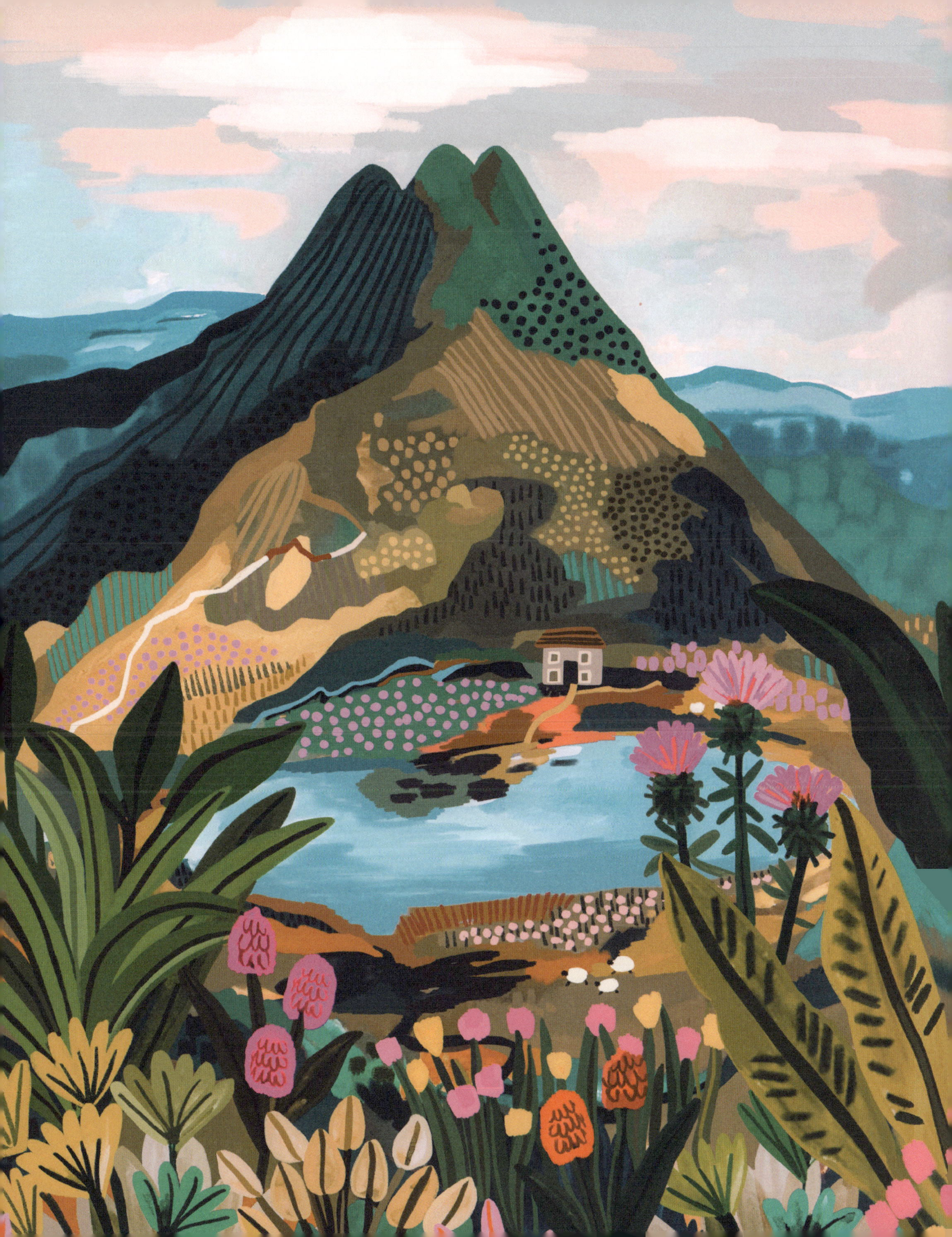

Snowdon, Wales

Not content with being the highest peak in Wales, Snowdon – Yr Wyddfa, in Welsh – is also home to extraordinary flora and fauna, as well as several lakes. If hiking isn't your thing, you can take the mountain railway – or you can paint your way to the top, taking in the mountain's variegated shades of green, grey and brown and the crystalline blue of its lakes.

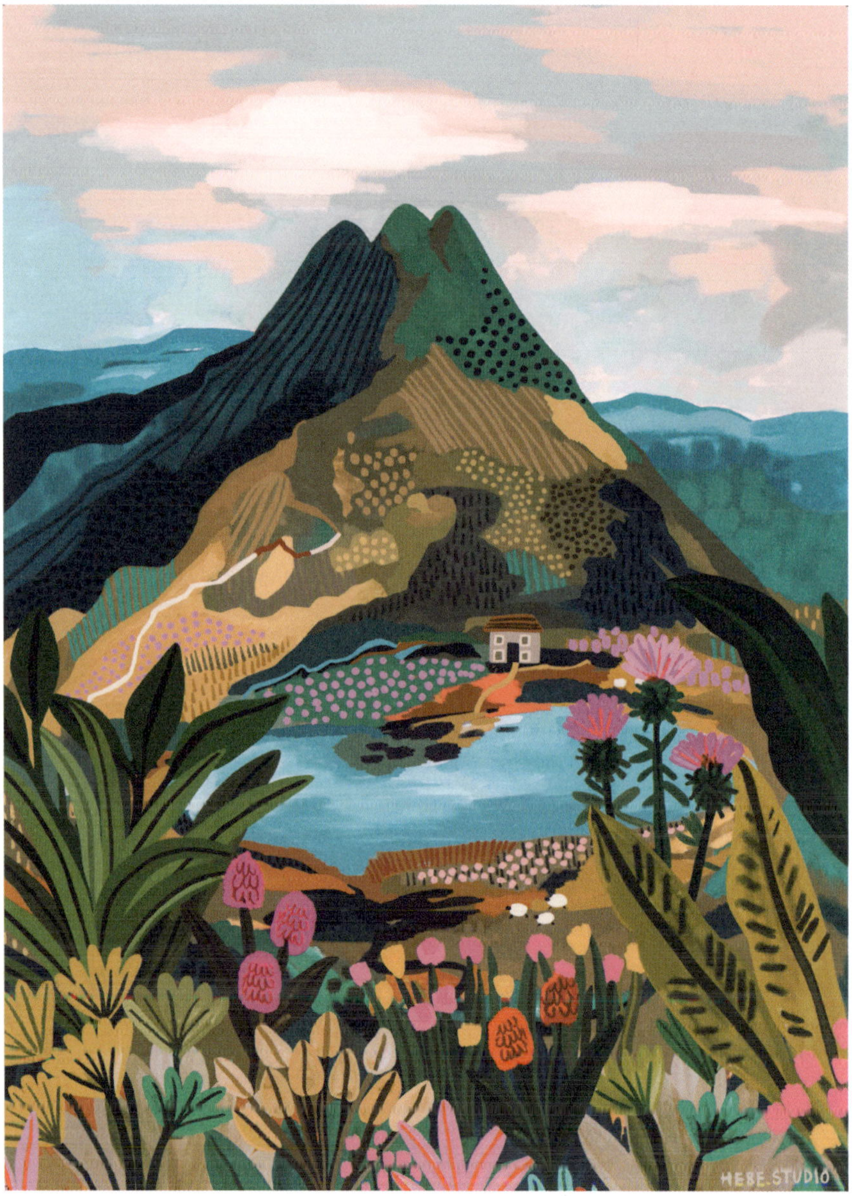

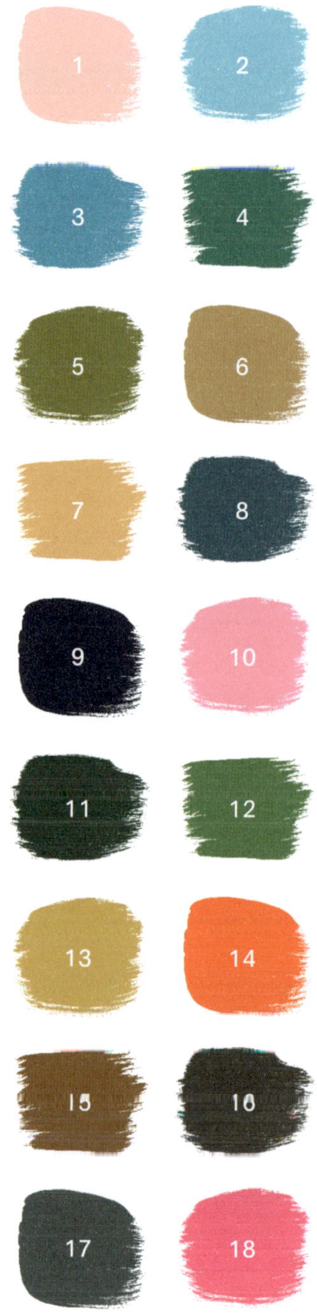

STEP BY STEP

- Start with the pastel shades of the sky
- Fill in the blue water
- Tackle the browns and greens of the mountain next
- Finish with the leaves, flowers and house

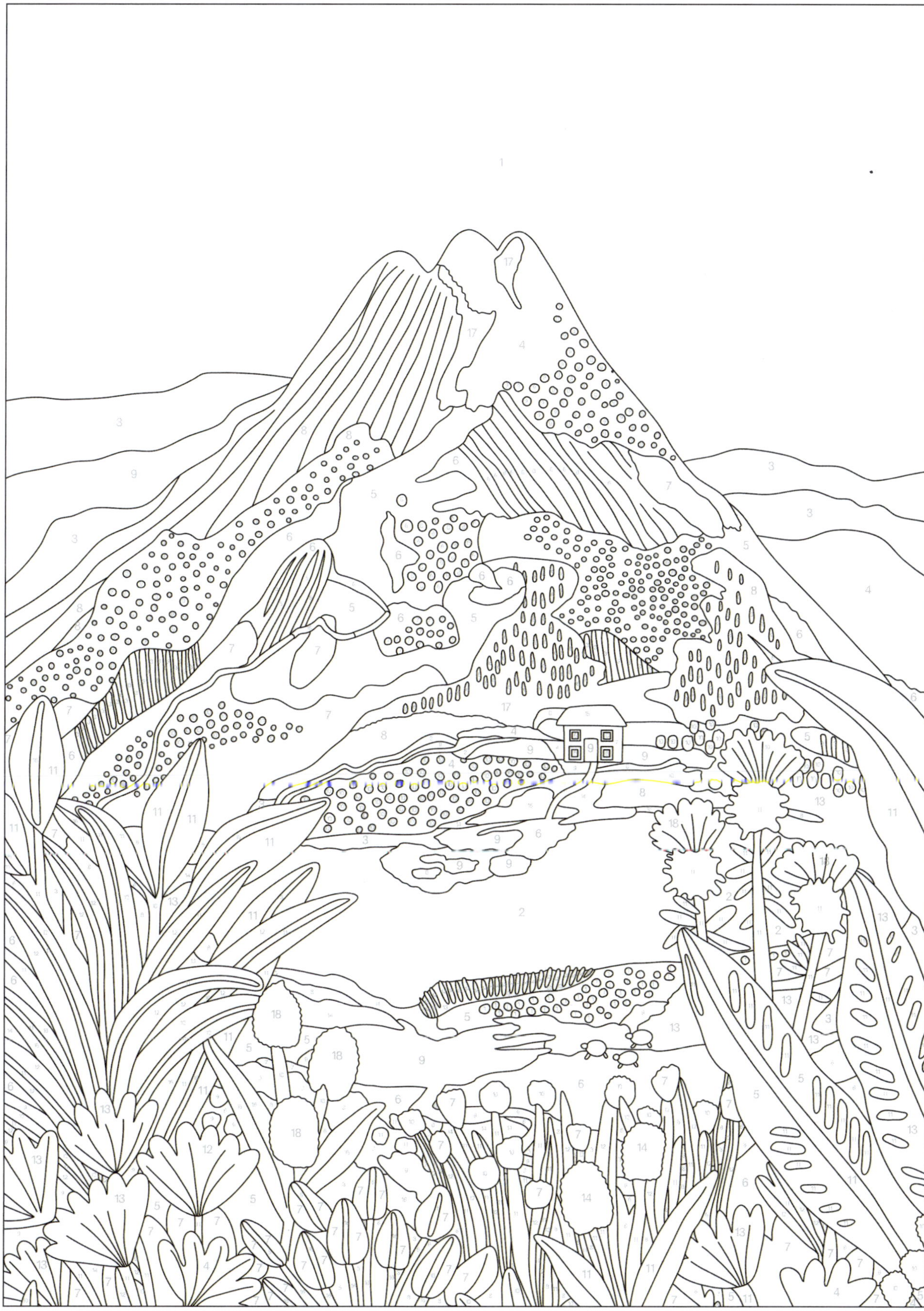

MARCHING ELEPHANTS, SRI LANKA

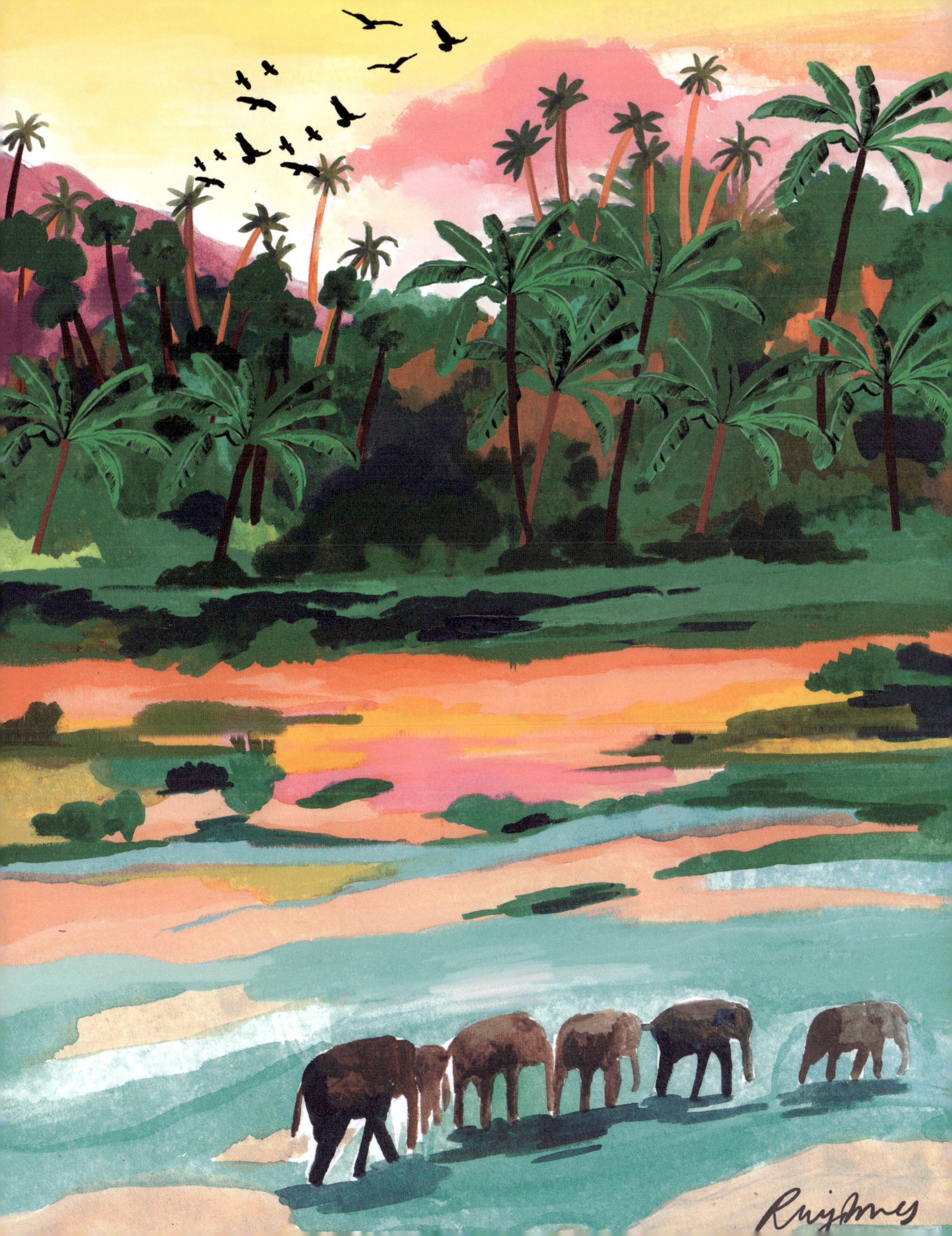

Marching Elephants, Sri Lanka

A backdrop of verdant green jungle, a patch of red-yellow soil, and, in the foreground, a welcome watering hole for a parade of elephants. The colors change with the depths of the painting – a powder blue at the bottom, moving to earthy colors and on into lush greens. The Sri Lankan sky is a mesmerizing smudge of yellows and pinks, casting a gentle light on the slow-moving elephants below.

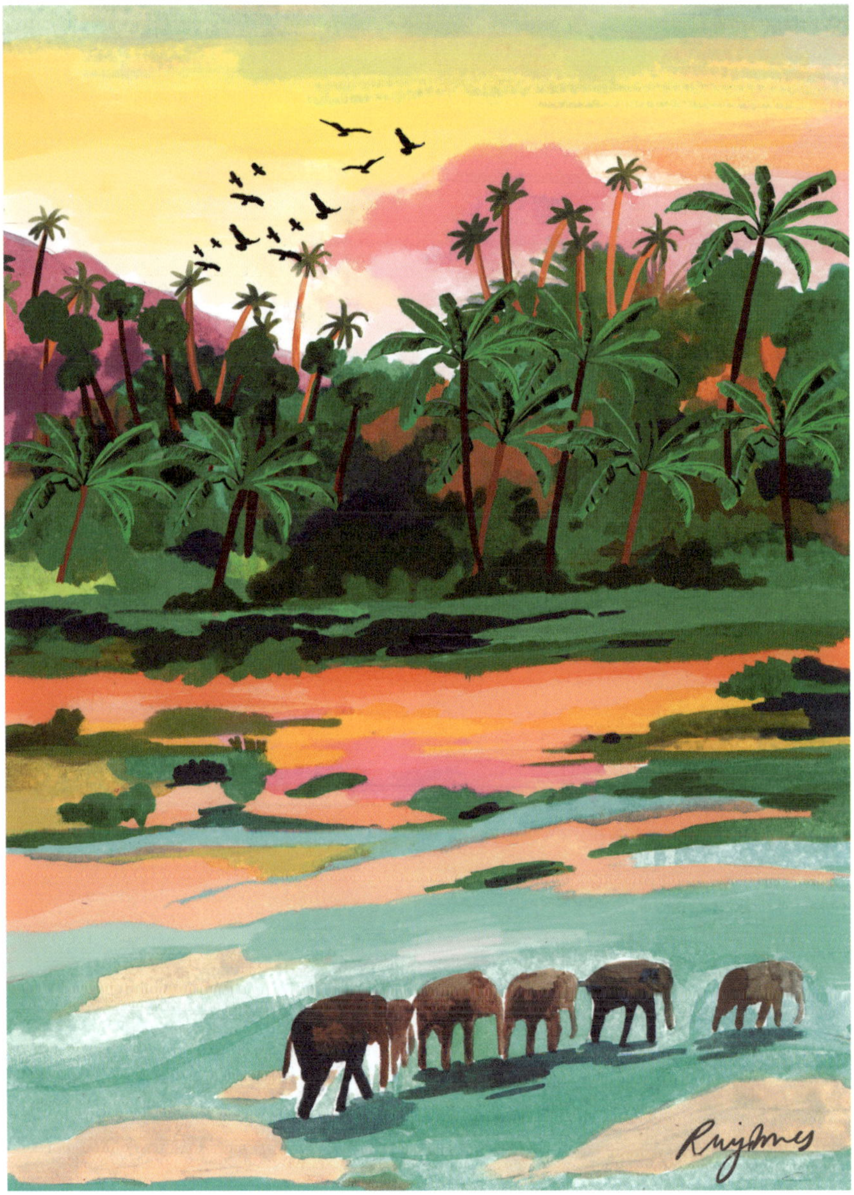

STEP BY STEP

- Start with the bruised colors of the sky
- Fill in the pinks, oranges and greens of the plains in the foreground
- Add all the greenery
- Finish with the elephants and birds

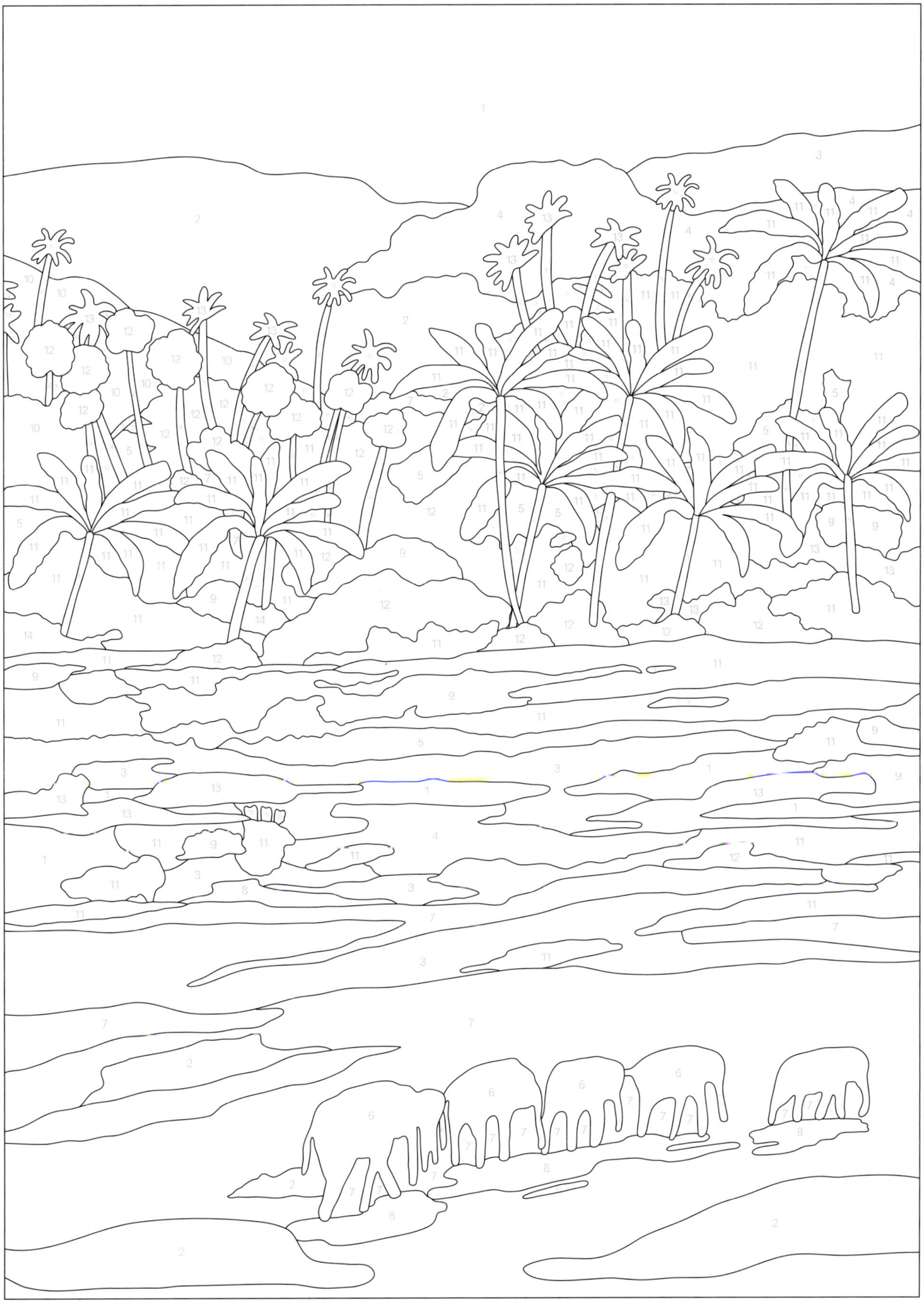

ROOFTOPS OF PARIS, FRANCE

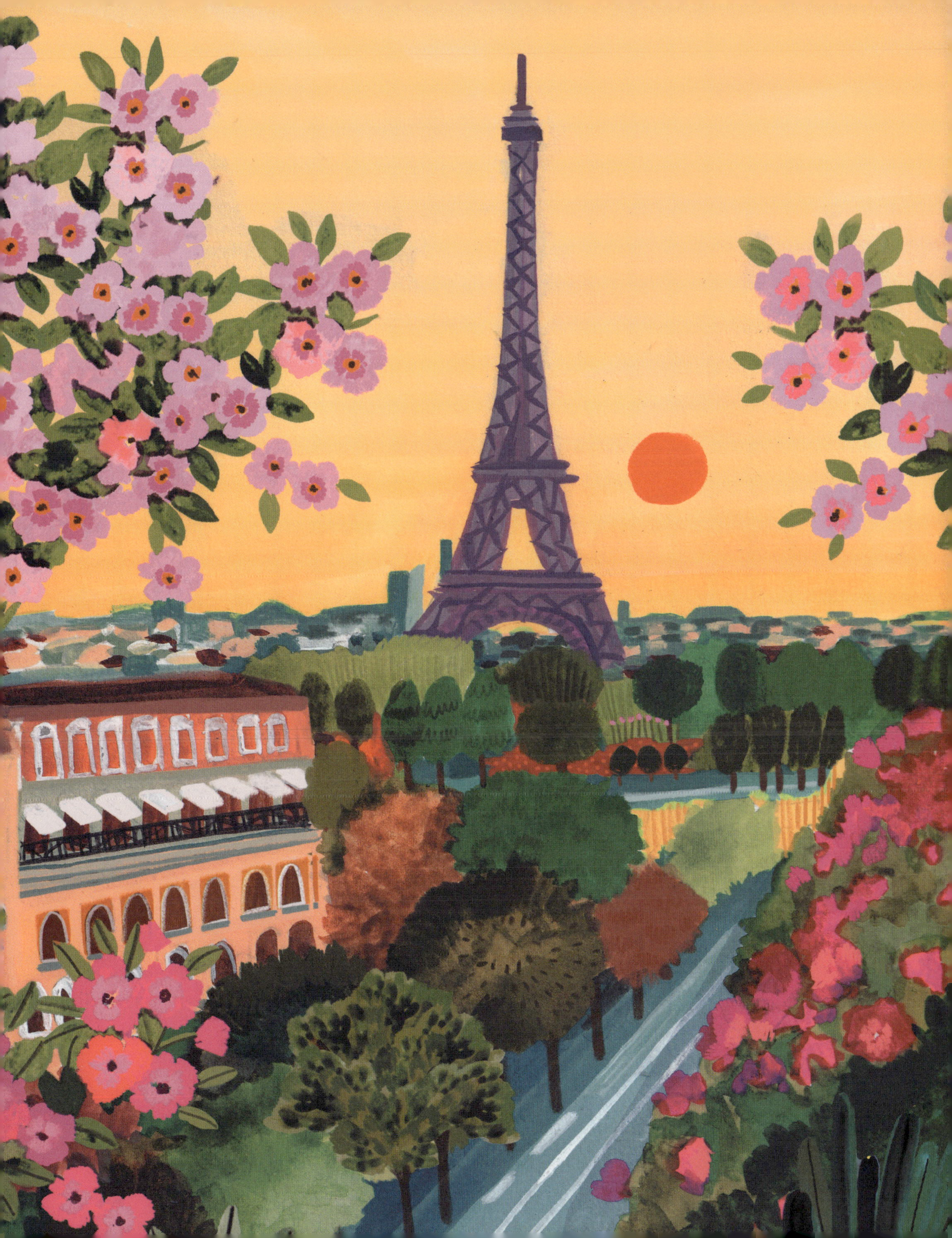

Rooftops of Paris, France

Imagine looking out at this scene from your balcony, glass of wine in hand, as the sun sets over the City of Lights and casts a magical golden glow. The cherry trees have burst into bloom and Paris is afire with spring life. Countless artists have immortalized Paris over the years; it's time for you to create your own picture-perfect postcard of tree-lined boulevards and, of course, the Eiffel Tower.

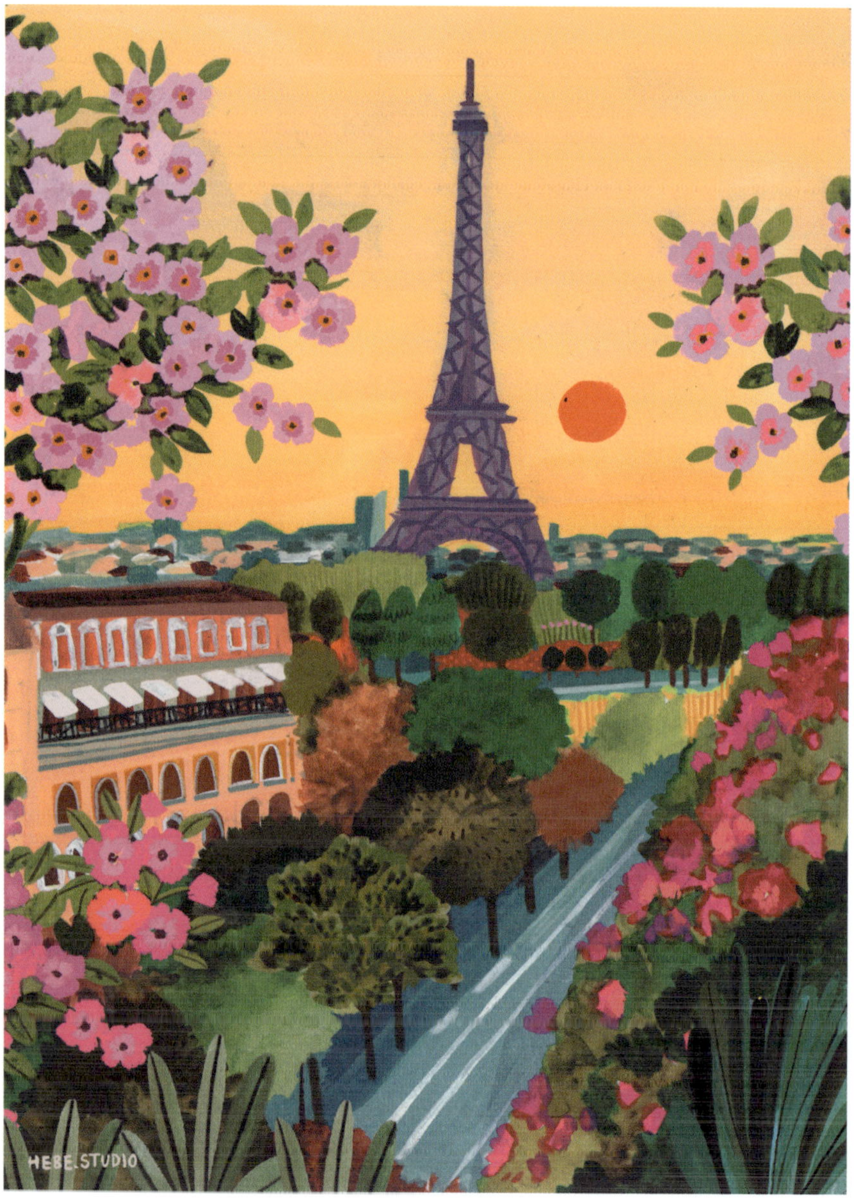

STEP BY STEP

- Start with the orange expanse of sky
- Tackle the Eiffel Tower next
- Fill in the greens of the trees and plants
- Finish with the flowers, building, road and sun

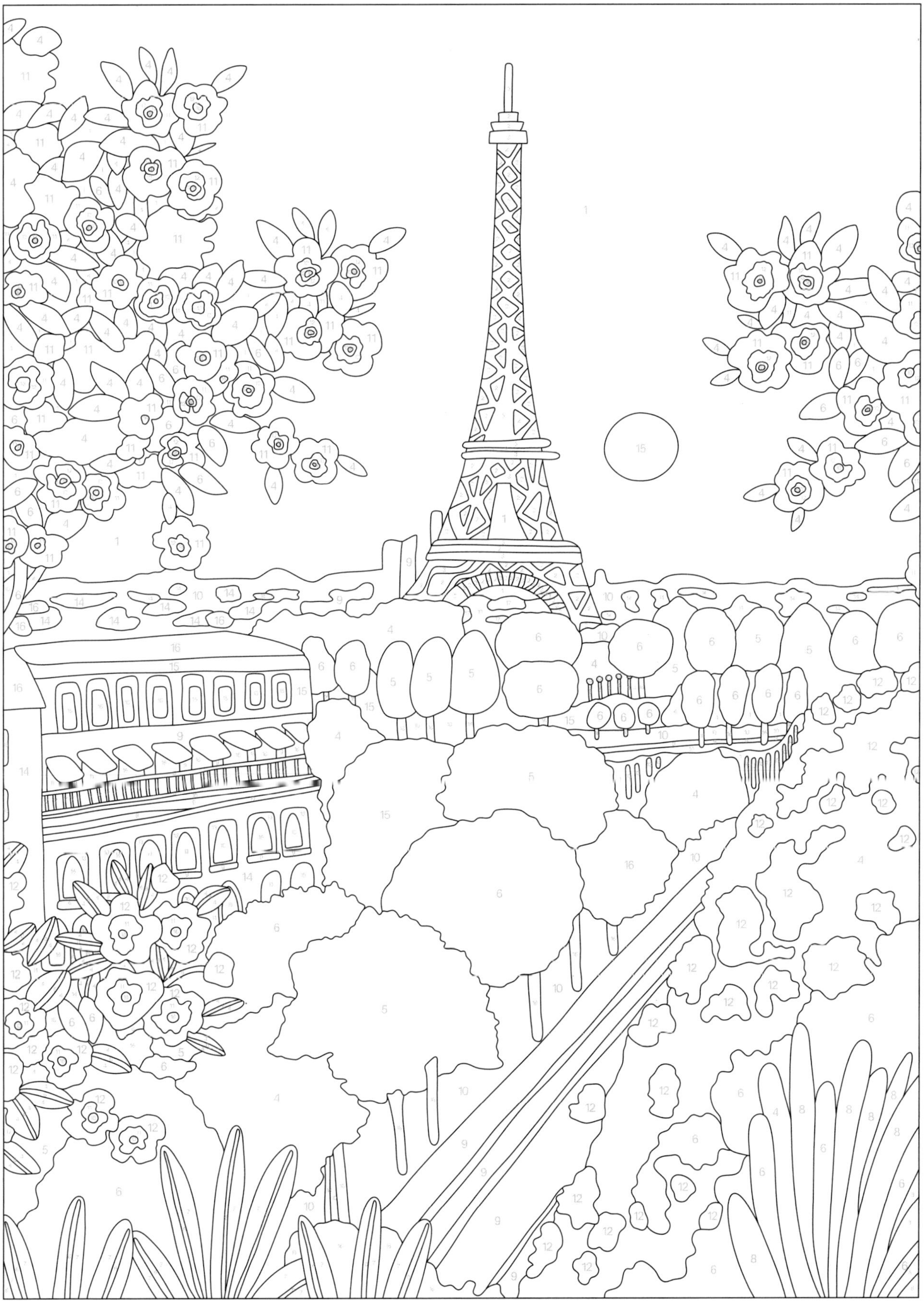

PORTO,
PORTUGAL

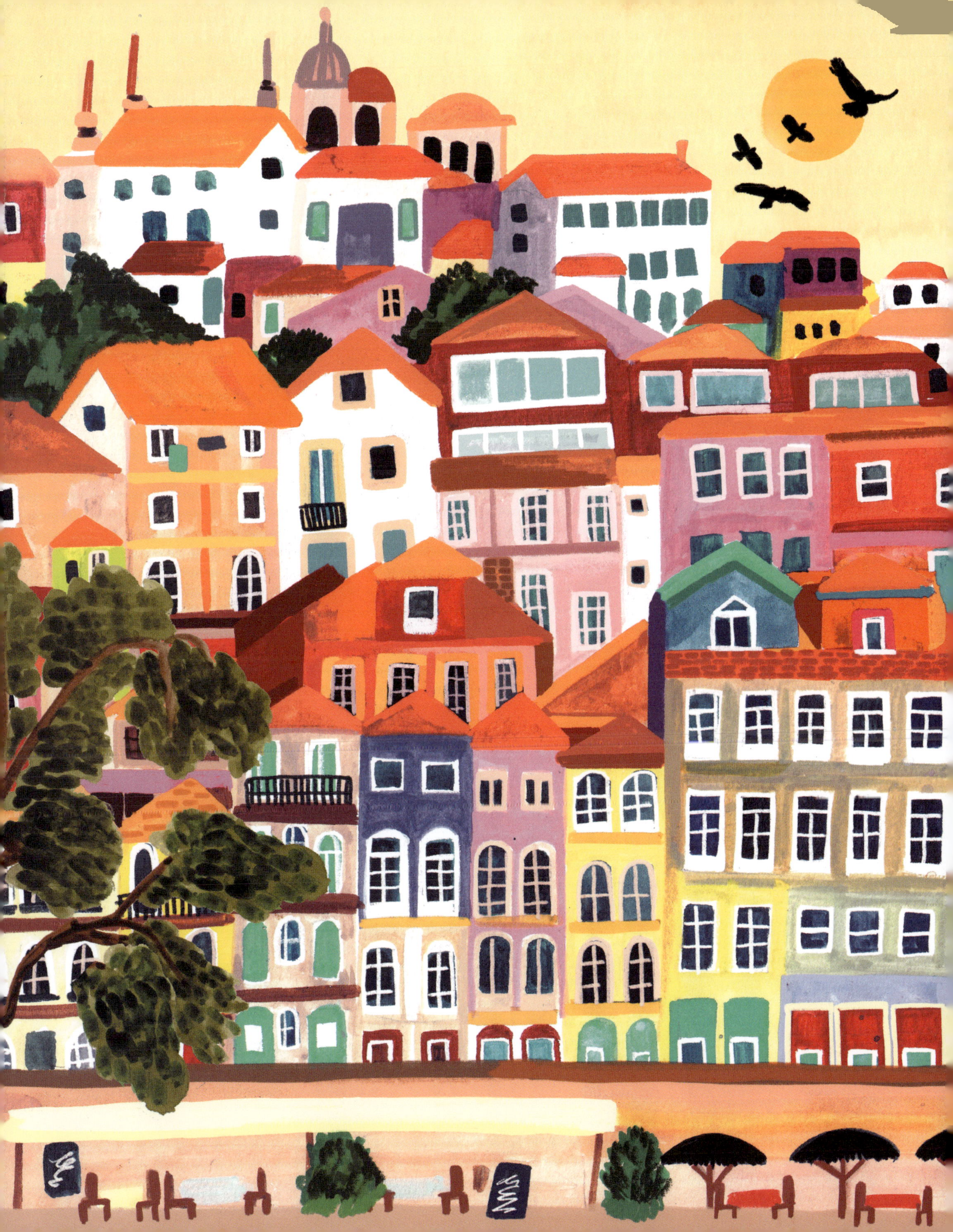

Porto, Portugal

Take your time painting each little window and rooftop of these iconic tall, narrow houses in Porto, overlooking the Douro river. Imagine strolling along the shaded medieval streets between the houses, trying some of the city's famous port, and taking a boat trip. Delight in the glorious architecture steeped in color, character and history – scenery that stays in the memory for a long time.

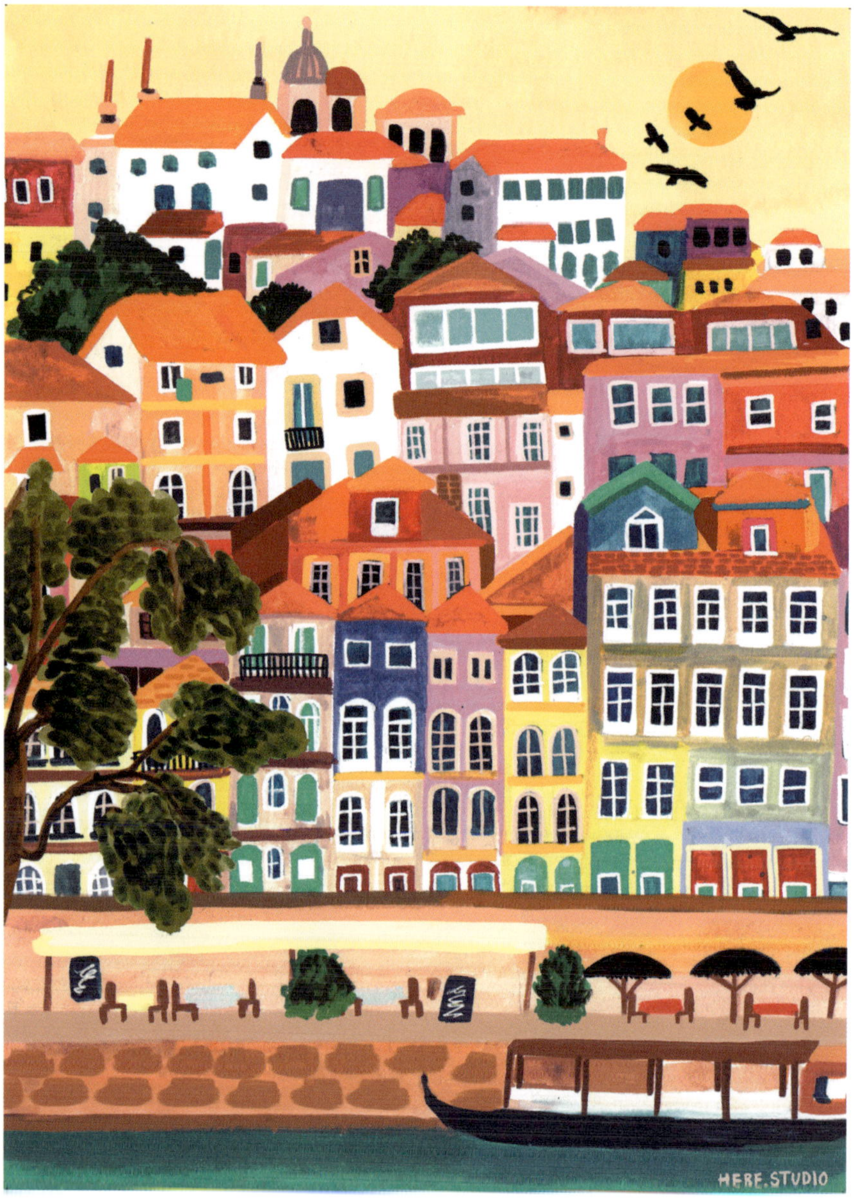

STEP BY STEP

- Start with the yellow of the sky
- Fill in the buildings and lower section of the picture
- Add the windows and roofs
- Finish with the greenery, birds, sun and other details

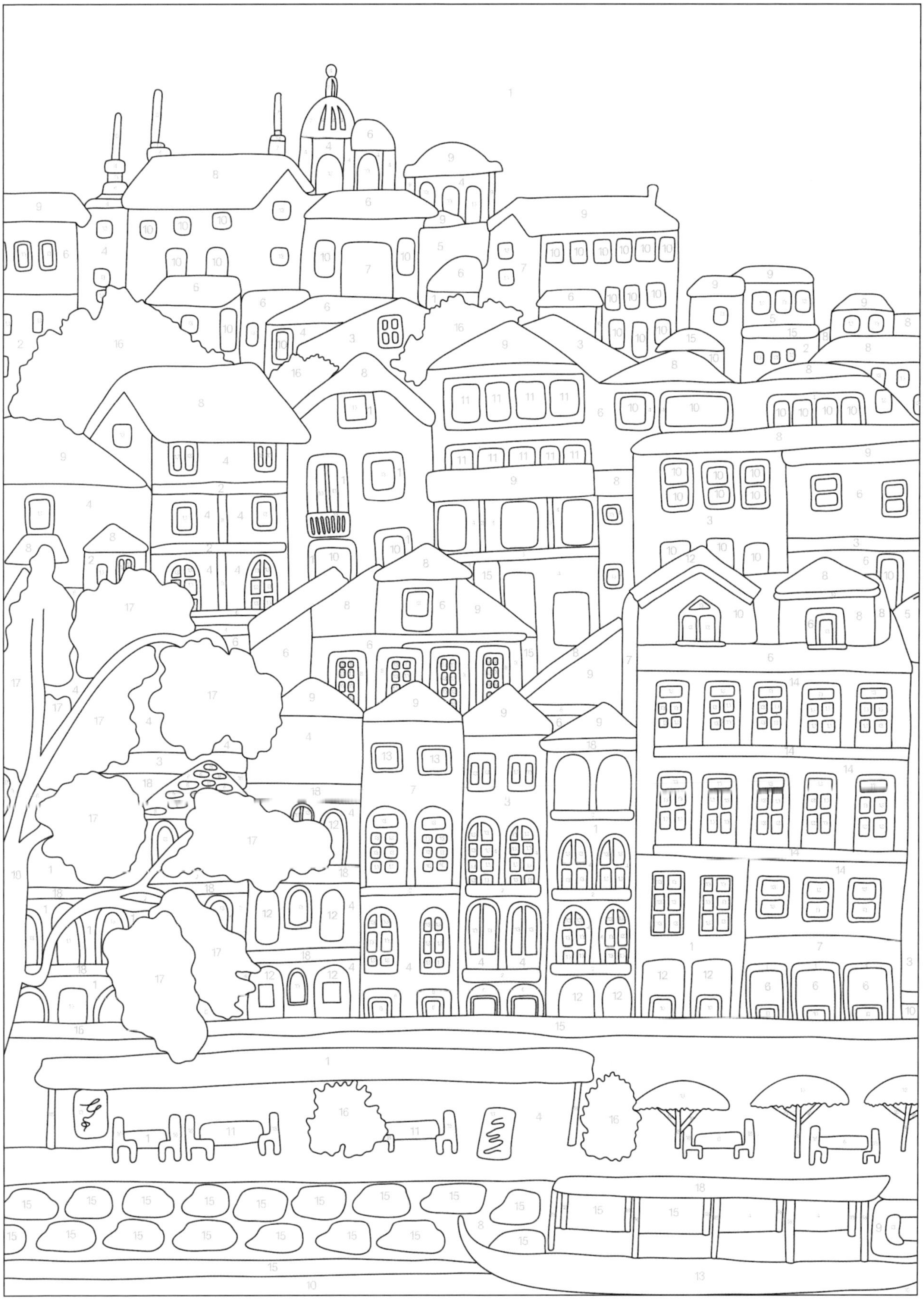

About the author & Hebe's story

Rhi James is a UK-born designer now based in Perth, Australia, and the founder of Hebe Studio. Established during the Covid pandemic, Hebe Studio grew from Rhi's love of travel and her ability to find beauty and inspiration in every corner of the world.

The studio was brought to life following a once-in-a-lifetime trip across India. On returning home, Rhi spent two weeks in quarantine painting – transforming her experiences into the vibrant, uplifting prints that define her work today. Her designs are created to inspire, uplift, and transport people to places near and far.

Today, Hebe Studio's artwork can be found across a wide range of products, including prints, calendars, planners, postcards, playing cards, and puzzles.

To explore more of Rhi's work, visit:
www.hebe.studio

You can also follow Hebe Studio on social media:

Instagram:
www.instagram.com/hebe.studio

TikTok:
www.tiktok.com/@hebe.studio

Facebook:
www.facebook.com/
Hebestudiostore

Pinterest:
www.uk.pinterest.com/
Hebestudiostore

Rhi would love to see your finished pieces. Share your pictures on social media, simply tag them with #artescapes and we can create a gallery of artworks inspired by travel!

Quadrille, Penguin Random House UK,
One Embassy Gardens, 8 Viaduct
Gardens, London SW11 7BW

Quadrille Publishing Limited is part of the Penguin Random House group of companies whose addresses can be found at global.penguinrandomhouse.com

Penguin Random House UK

Published by Quadrille in 2026
www.penguin.co.uk

A CIP catalogue record for this book is available from the British Library

ISBN 978 1807 12092 4

10 9 8 7 6 5 4 3 2 1

Managing Director Sarah Lavelle
Editorial Director Harriet Butt
Copy Editor Céline Hughes
Design Manager Katherine Case
Senior Designer Emily Lapworth
Artworker Sarah Fisher
Head of Production Stephen Lang
Color reproduction by F1

Printed in China by C&C
Offset Printing Co., Ltd.

The authorized representative in the EEA is Penguin Random House Ireland, Morrison Chambers, 32 Nassau Street, Dublin D02 YH68.

FSC
www.fsc.org
MIX
Paper
FSC® C018179

Penguin Random House is committed to a sustainable future for our business, our readers and our planet. This book is made from Forest Stewardship Council® certified paper.

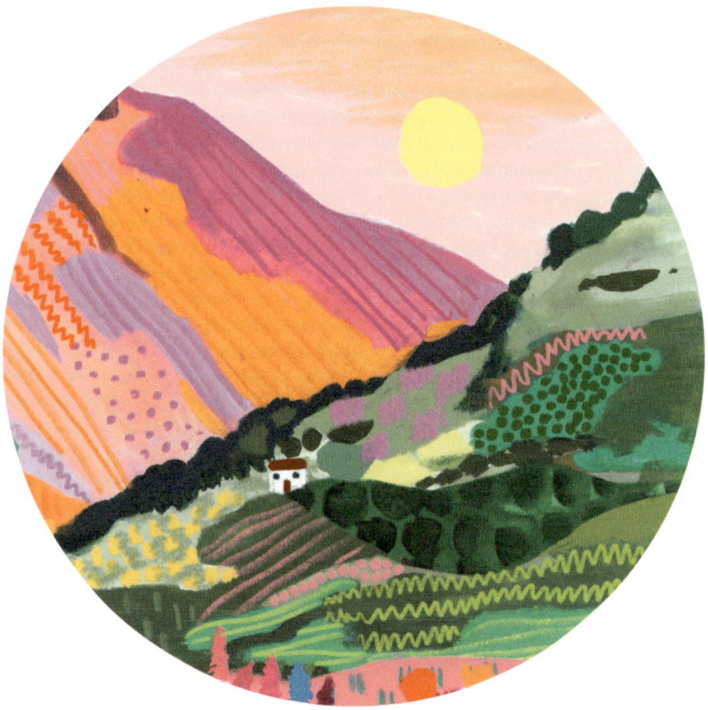